Strategic Journeys for Building Logical Reasoning, 9–12

Help your students develop logical reasoning and critical thinking skills. This new book from bestselling authors and popular consultants Tammy Jones and Leslie Texas offers authentic logic-building activities and writing strategies that can be used across all subject areas in grades 9–12. Filled with hands-on activities and photocopiable tools, *Strategic Journeys* will help you guide students into deeper thinking to go beyond the surface of content to true understanding.

Topics include:

◆ Identifying opportunities for students to engage in meaningful and relevant writing across the content areas;
◆ Introducing a logical reasoning process, questioning structure, and bridging models to allow students to delve deeper into problems;
◆ Incorporating literature to increase student engagement and make content come alive for your students;
◆ Building vocabulary and literacy skills through fun activities aimed at increasing proficiency;
◆ Using the Three Phases of Logical Reasoning to plan lessons effectively, help students reflect on their progress, and implement the strategies successfully.

The strategies in this book have been implemented in hundreds of classrooms around the country, and have been proven to increase student engagement, promote higher-order thinking and in-depth reasoning, and improve overall achievement.

Tammy L. Jones has been an educator since 1979, working with students from first grade through college. She currently consults with individual school districts to support teachers in making content accessible to all students.

Leslie A. Texas has over 20 years of experience working with K–12 teachers and schools across the country to enhance rigorous and relevant instruction.

Strategic Journeys for Building Logical Reasoning, 9–12

Activities Across the Content Areas

Tammy L. Jones and Leslie A. Texas

 Routledge
Taylor & Francis Group

NEW YORK AND LONDON

First published 2017
by Routledge
711 Third Avenue, New York, NY 10017

and by Routledge
2 Park Square, Milton Park, Abingdon, Oxon, OX14 4RN

Routledge is an imprint of the Taylor & Francis Group, an informa business

Library of Congress Cataloging-in-Publication Data
Names: Jones, Tammy L., author. | Texas, Leslie A., author.
Title: Strategic journeys for building logical reasoning, 9–12 :
   activities across the content areas / by Tammy Jones and Leslie Texas.
Description: New York, NY : Routledge, 2016. | Series: Strategic
   journeys series | Includes bibliographical references.
Identifiers: LCCN 2016004037 | ISBN 9781138932449 (hardback) |
   ISBN 9781138932456 (pbk.) | ISBN 9781315679259 (e-book)
Subjects: LCSH: Thought and thinking—Study and teaching
   (Secondary)—Activity programs. | Critical thinking—Study
   and teaching (Secondary)—Activity programs. | Content area
   reading. | Cognition in children.
Classification: LCC LB1590.3 .J659 2016 | DDC 370.15/2—dc23
LC record available at https://lccn.loc.gov/2016004037

ISBN: 978-1-138-93244-9 (hbk)
ISBN: 978-1-138-93245-6 (pbk)
ISBN: 978-1-315-67925-9 (ebk)

Typeset in Palatino
by Apex CoVantage, LLC

Contents

eResources

As you read this book, you'll notice the eResources icon (🌐) next to the following tools. The icon indicates that these tools are available as free downloads on our website, www.routledge.com/9781138932456, so you can easily print and distribute them to your students.

Tools

In addition, if you'd like color versions of the Q-Pyramid or other tools in this book, or a Q-Pyramid and posters for students, please contact the authors at info@TexasAndJones.com.

Meet the Authors

Collectively Tammy and Leslie have almost 40 years of classroom experience teaching in elementary, middle, and high school. This has included urban, suburban, rural, and private school settings. Being active members of their professional organizations has allowed them to continually grow professionally and model lifelong learning for both their students and their peers. In their twenty-plus years of combined consulting work, they have had opportunities to work with teachers and students from kindergarten through college level. This work has spanned almost all 50 states. Their work has included helping to develop standards and curriculum at the state level as well as implementing curriculum and best practice strategies at the classroom level. One of the things that sets Tammy and Leslie apart as consultants is their work with classroom teachers, modeling and offering continued support throughout the year to build capacity at the building and district levels. Tammy and Leslie co-authored the 2013 series from Eye On Education/ Routledge-Taylor & Francis Group, *Strategies for Common Core Standards for Mathematics: Implementing the Standards for Mathematical Practice* (Grades K–5, 6–8, and 9–12).

An educator since 1979, **Tammy L. Jones** has worked with students from first grade through college. Currently, Tammy is consulting with individual school districts in training teachers on strategies for making content accessible to all learners. Writing integrations as well as literacy connections are foundational in everything Tammy does. Tammy also works with teachers on effective techniques for being successful in the classroom. As a classroom teacher, Tammy's goal was that all students understand and appreciate the content they were studying; that they could read it, write it, explore it, and communicate it with confidence; and that they would be able to use the content as they need to in their lives. She believes that logical reasoning, followed by a well-reasoned presentation of results, is central to the process of learning, and that this learning happens most effectively in a cooperative, student-centered classroom. Tammy believes that learning is experiential and in her current consulting work creates and shares engaging and effective educational experiences.

Leslie A. Texas has over 20 years of experience working with K–12 teachers and schools across the country to enhance rigorous and relevant instruction. She believes that improving student outcomes depends on comprehensive approaches to teaching and learning. She taught middle and high school mathematics and science, and has strong content expertise in both areas. Through her advanced degree studies, she honed her skills in content and program development and student-centered instruction. Using a combination of direct instruction, modeling, and problem-solving activities rooted in practical application, Leslie helps teachers become more effective classroom leaders and peer coaches.

Preface

A Note to Our Readers

In our first book series, *Strategies for Common Core Mathematics: Implementing the Standards for Mathematical Practice K–5, 6–8,* and *9–12*, we shared practical ideas on how to engage students in mathematical practices, develop problem-solving skills, and promote higher-order thinking. We opened that series by asking questions we thought our readers might have and then provided the answers to those questions. The positive feedback was so overwhelming that we agreed to do the same with this series, posing some of the same questions as well as a new one. This is intended to illustrate how this series has grown from the last. Our passion and focus remains the same, but we have broadened the audience to help build a community of educators all working toward empowering students to be independent thinkers and to possess appropriate logical reasoning skills.

When we took on the task of writing this new series, we asked ourselves two questions: **So what**? and **Who cares**? Why write a book about developing logical reasoning and how could we do it in such a way that would make a difference? These were the questions that guided our process as we developed the materials contained within these pages. Practical, versatile, easy to implement, maximizing student engagement, and yielding results—these were the criteria we used as a guideline for selecting the strategies for this book. Other questions we thought might be of interest, as well as our responses, are listed below:

Why are the same strategies used in all three books in the series?
We intentionally chose strategies versatile enough to be used across the grade levels so we could illustrate the progression of concept development that occurs within and across subject areas. Explicitly illustrating the scaffolding of skills across grade level and content boundaries emphasizes the importance of developing the overarching practices students need to be successful. Check out the Opportunities for Writing Task Alignment in Appendix B and the Strategies with Task Alignment in Appendix C.

How can I teach all my content standards using the strategies in this book?
All the strategies contained in this book are versatile and can be used with any content standards you choose. We have included content-specific examples

to illustrate how the strategy works, but none of the strategies are limited to the concepts shown. There is also one sample task that can be used as a beginning point for an interdisciplinary Project-Based Learning experience.

How do I know these strategies will work in my classroom?

These are proven strategies that have been implemented in our own classrooms as well as in hundreds of classrooms around the country. They were intentionally chosen based on their ease of use and the impact they have had on student engagement and achievement. Some of the strategies were shared by teachers with whom we work; permission for their use has been given.

How can I develop independent thinkers and provide an opportunity for fluency?

Students must be able to engage in discourse using their understanding and knowledge of the content. In order to gain mastery, they need to practice the skills. This book contains specific strategies that illustrate how to engage students in developing key content practices as well as additional strategies to promote higher-order thinking and in-depth reasoning in Chapter 3 (The Journey to Deeper Understandings: Building Practices). Knowing that teachers still need strategies to engage students as they are building procedural fluency and content knowledge, Chapter 4 (The Journey from Practice to Proficiency: Strategies that Engage) includes several examples that teachers can adapt for their specific needs.

Why would I buy this book?

The value of this book is that it not only contains strategies to prepare students for these rigorous assessments, but it also provides practical notes on how to implement them effectively. In addition, we share specific tools that can be used to scaffold students' development of logical reasoning over time and allow them to become **independent thinkers** that don't rely on the teacher to tell them what to do.

Why read the introductory chapters instead of going directly to the tasks pages?

Chapter 1 outlines all of the powerful tools available and how they are integrated together for a comprehensive approach to developing logical reasoning. Chapter 2 details the importance of authentic writing and explains the types we reference with each task in Chapter 3. If you skip these chapters, you will probably end up going back to understand all of the elements and how they fit together.

By answering these questions, we hope to have modeled best practice instruction by hooking you into wanting to learn what it is we have to share in this book. Now let us begin the journey.

1

Why This Journey?

More rigorous standards in all disciplines and at all grade levels, a greater emphasis on writing and communication, a need for support with effective questioning, and strategies to engage students as they practice to develop proficiencies. These are but a few of the challenges facing today's educators as they are tasked with making content accessible to all students.

This book series shares strategies and resources that have proved successful with students at all ages and levels. Several of these strategies were first shared in our previous series, *Strategies for Common Core Mathematics: Implementing the Standards for Mathematical Practice*. We realized how the strategies we shared in that series could be used in all disciplines and across all grade bands as our work extended beyond mathematics. Out of that work, we have developed some new tools and redesigned some old ones. *Strategic Journeys for Building Logical Reasoning, K–12: Activities Across the Content Areas* introduces the Journey's Notebook, the Logical Reasoning Process, and the Q-Pyramid as universal tools to aid both students and teachers in being successful with the current more rigorous standards and next generation of assessments. This series includes:

- ◆ Charting the Course: Communicating the Journey
- ◆ The Journey to Deeper Understandings: Building Practices
- ◆ The Journey from Practice to Proficiency: Strategies that Engage
- ◆ Navigating the Journey: Staying the Course

One of the biggest challenges facing today's educators is addressing more rigorous standards that have now been adopted by many states. Students are required to develop deeper understandings of their content and to communicate that understanding. For that reason, this book begins with an emphasis on writing and communication. Writing about your thinking is one of the main shifts in today's instruction and the next generation of assessments. All teachers, not just ELA teachers, need to provide students opportunities to authentically engage in writing and communication in support of the work that ELA teachers have before them. Knowing that the next generation of assessments is placing a much greater demand on writing from today's students, it is imperative that teachers in all disciplines at all grade levels incorporate authentic writing opportunities in their classrooms. Chapter 2 shares seven natural opportunities for students to engage in meaningful and relevant writing and provides specific interdisciplinary examples for each. The Journey's Notebook is introduced as a way to chronicle the journey a student makes and capture the student's writing. These opportunities permeate all of the other topics throughout the book. These include writing as a tool for showing evidence, reflecting, creating ideas, inquiry, making meaning, educating, and producing products. Vocabulary strategies are embedded in each of these components as well. Many of the black line masters can be formatted for standalone use or for use in a composition-type book that students might use as their Journey's Notebooks. Several writing prompts are included.

> It is imperative that teachers in all disciplines at all grade levels incorporate authentic writing opportunities in their classrooms.

Whether it is a contextual problem to solve in mathematics, a scientific investigation to perform, a piece of text to analyze, or historical events to interpret, students are engaging in logical reasoning. In Chapter 3, we propose some tools that have proved to be successful in meeting the challenge. These tools include a logical reasoning process, a questioning structure, and bridging models that allow students to learn to create questions themselves.

Any structure built needs a good foundation. The foundation for effectively communicating the results of engaging with these tools is writing. In every sample task, opportunities for writing will be shared. A beginning trade book list will also be provided. Trade books definitely have a place in today's classroom! Incorporating literature into the classroom at any level can increase student engagement, make the content being studied come alive and have meaning for the student, and help to differentiate instruction as well as support ELL/ESL students. Using literature helps students build a conceptual understanding of topics via the illustrations. Rich problems and tasks can be generated based upon the story being read—as well as opportunities for writing original stories, explanations, predictions, and so on. Reading stories sparks a student's imagination and allows them to see a context for a problem or situation and visualize it in a way that the same problem in a textbook or on a worksheet might not. Using literature also bridges the gap for students who are verbal learners and who love to read but may not enjoy working with the specific content as much.

Tools

◆ logical reasoning process,
◆ a questioning structure, and
◆ bridging models that allow students to learn to create questions themselves.

Revisiting Puzzling Problems is a nonthreatening way to engage students in the problem/context/scenario that illustrates how to make difficult content accessible to more students. The Logical Reasoning Process (LRP) offers a structure in which students can first begin to work with these more challenging situations. Knowing that effective questioning is the foundation for successful implementation of any task in the classroom, we have identified four **opportunities for questioning**. Integrative questioning and the Q-Pyramid are introduced as tools to aid in developing effective questioning. Students can even use the overlay to create questions on their own to help move them. This tool has proved to be invaluable as teachers face differentiating their instruction. Through the deliberate and thoughtful preparation of questions, especially the reflection and extension, even the upper level of student, who is often neglected, can now be challenged with authentic extensions instead of being punished by simply being given more things to do.

Every discipline at every level has basic factual content, knowledge, and procedural information that students need to learn and demonstrate proficiency. In Chapter 4, we revisit updated versions of Matching Mania, Grid Games, and the ABC Sum Race. The Multiple Representation Match is introduced, as well as several other new strategies to use while building vocabulary and literacy. All of these strategies provide a nonthreatening and engaging environment for students to practice skills while building proficiency. These work very well for small group, learning station, and center activities.

The Three Phases of Logical Reasoning are discussed in Chapters 3 and 5 as a structure to guide both the teacher and the student in what successful implementation of these tools involves. It also serves as a guide for administrators in gathering evidence during teacher observations. The beauty of these tools is that they were developed to connect and support one another. We have developed a graphic that visually makes these connections.

Connecting the four opportunities for questioning to the LRP resulted in the creation of a powerful tool—the **Q-Pyramid and an Overlay**. Even primary teachers are using the overlay as an aid for creating questions on the fly. Students and teachers are using the Q-Pyramid to connect where they are in the Logical Reasoning Process and as a tool to support moving the learning and the learner forward.

Materials are provided in the Appendices so educators can easily implement and adapt the strategies and resources shared.

- Appendix A offers black line masters and information about the Logical Reasoning Process, the sample tasks used in Chapter 3, and the task-specific questions modeling the opportunities for questioning.
- Appendix B offers a variety of writing samples for the seven opportunities for writing, as well as facilitation notes and sample reflections to aid the teacher in the implementation of the strategies.
- Appendix C provides the black line masters of activities from Chapter 4, which offer an engaging way to provide practice for students as they work toward building fluency.
- Appendix D is a resource for the content-specific practices from the four academic disciplines: mathematics, ELA, science, and social studies.

2

Charting the Course: Communicating the Journey

As stated earlier, the next generation of assessments is placing a much greater demand on writing from today's students. So it is imperative that teachers in all disciplines at all grade levels incorporate authentic writing opportunities in their classrooms. Because of the way today's educational system is structured, students often perceive English class as English class and math class as something different. They ask, "Why would I dare bring something that occurs in English class into math class?" Everything seems to be so compartmentalized. Even in the elementary grades that are still self-contained, schedules often dictate a specific time for subjects to begin and end, often with little flexibility.

"Literacy across the curriculum" means that we incorporate reading and writing as a natural component of our content-specific courses rather than by forcing compliance. For example, if we are having students write about how they solved a problem when it is obvious from the mathematical steps, this is redundant. Instead, we can ask students to go further by writing about why they chose the strategy they did versus another strategy or by stating what properties they employed as evidence to support the computations they performed. This example highlights mathematics in ELA but also applies to science, social studies, and CTE (Career Technical Education).

Writing is a journey that students and educators take individually and together. Evidence that students can speak about something does not demonstrate that they can also write about it. *Talking about* and *writing about* are two completely different skill sets. There are various purposes and opportunities that are available in each discipline for writing. This section focuses on exploring seven natural opportunities for students to engage in meaningful and relevant writing. Specific interdisciplinary examples for each are included here as well as in Chapter 3 and Chapter 4. Every discipline has opportunities to use writing for specific purposes. There are seven opportunities for authentic writing that occur regularly in most disciplines (Figure 2.1).

Talking about and *writing about* are two completely different skill sets.

Figure 2.1 Seven Opportunities for Authentic Writing

This list is neither linear nor cyclical because we find these are interconnected more often than not in the classroom. These seven opportunities are:

Making Meaning—understanding the question posed and identifying given and needed information necessary to proceed
Showing Evidence—using facts and/or data to support one's argument/hypothesis/work
Reflecting—being metacognitive with respect to strategies and/or processes
Inquiry—creating questions to drive investigation and/or research
Educating—informing others in various forms and for various purposes—persuasive, descriptive, expository, and narrative
Creating Ideas—brainstorming/free writing to begin framing ideas
Producing Products—using products to convey a message, depending on audience and purpose (research papers, proposals, brochures, essays, public service announcements, etc.)

Many teachers ask, "Where should I start?" Using writing as a way of showing evidence and writing as a tool of reflection will support an increase in student achievement in the classroom. Three forms of showing evidence include: evidence of prior knowledge, evidence in supporting an argument, and evidence of understanding.

Pre-assessing or benchmarking where students are in their journey through a specific discipline, assessing, diagnosing, and prescribing on the fly are daily requirements of today's educator at any level. One of the most basic ways to accomplish this is with the Glossary in My Journey's Notebook. (More on My Journey's Notebook will be discussed at the end of this chapter.) As a new topic is introduced—for example, algebra in the eighth grade—have students go to the "A" page of their Glossary to write the word and what they understand about the term. IDK (I don't know) is not allowed.

I don't know versus *I don't care*: A blank piece of paper does not distinguish between the two. There are strategies to support *IDK* but a different set to support *I don't care.*

Remind students that when you said the term a thought flew through their minds. Tell them to go catch it and write it down. Students need to understand that there is no right or wrong answer at this beginning stage. This is an opportunity to begin effective discourse about the topic and gather evidence of prior knowledge and understanding. Teachers have to be very intentional and deliberate in how they facilitate this discourse. As students are writing, the teacher has the opportunity to walk around the room and see what types of responses are being given. If a **timed writing** strategy is used, the student who immediately raises a hand knows that, until time is up, no one is going to be called upon. This allows the opportunity to call upon a student who is struggling and has perhaps not answered a question all year but has a beginning idea for this topic.

> **Timed writing:** Giving students a specific amount of time to write about a topic. During this time, they must be writing. Depending upon the topic, students can also use some diagrams, pictures, or other approaches applicable to the topic.

Consider a familiar scenario: A class is asked to write in their Glossaries what they know about algebra, and one young lady immediately shoots up her hand. If the young lady is initially called upon, the rest of the conversation will most likely shut down. But if students are given time to think and write, then the teacher can choose a student who rarely volunteers to answer a question. Even if he has written, "Algebra is a course I will take in high school," that is a place to start discourse by asking, "So what is that course going to look like?" Now a conversation can begin about some components of algebra that you have written down. Along the way, teachers are monitoring for misconceptions as students are guided to annotate their responses. Students do not erase or whiteout; they strike through what needs to be corrected or restated more precisely. They add to their responses before coming to consensus as a class. This is a beginning place that offers the simplest of ways to assess where your students are as you start the study of a topic.

A second way of showing evidence is through argumentation. This is the way of showing evidence that most teachers in today's educational landscape think about. Today's students are asked to justify their work, cite evidence in support of their position, and validate their conclusions. This is one of the practices that is included in the Common Core Standards for Mathematical Practices as well as the Common Core ELA Student Portraits. The Next Generation of Science Standards and the C3 Framework for Social Studies Standards both include practices for argumentation, reporting out, and showing evidence. (See Chapter 3 for a list of each of the Practices for each of the four disciplines.) Students need opportunities to construct viable arguments and provide evidence in support of their thinking. Whether in mathematics, verifying why 4 can be added to both sides of an equation; in U.S. History, citing a primary source such as the U.S. Constitution in support of an argument;

or in science, performing an experiment and reporting the data to support a hypothesis—students must be able to communicate through writing to show evidence. These are skills that students today need to be successful in careers and life. Communication and writing permeate everything.

Communication and writing permeate everything.

Evidence of understanding for a teacher is *what the teacher sees* from students that lets them know that the student has the required knowledge and understanding of the topic at hand. Evidence of understanding for a student is *what the student knows that they are doing* that allows them to know what they know. Too often teachers fail to ask, "How do my students know that they know?"

How do your students know that they know?

Frayer Models (with examples and counterexamples) can be effective organizers for students to show evidence of understanding of foundational academic vocabulary terms (Figure 2.2). Using a Frayer Model is a nonthreatening way

Figure 2.2 Frayer Model. A reproducible version of this tool is available in Appendix B (p. 107).

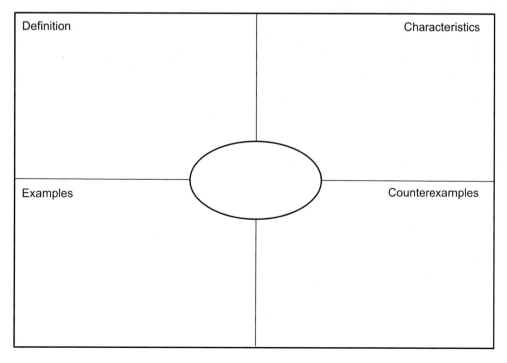

to get students to begin putting words to paper—to start writing. As a **note-taking guide,** this organizational tool helps students frame their thinking around the key components needed to develop understanding of main vocabulary terms.

There are a few variations on the traditional Frayer Model. Reverse Frayer is using a completed Frayer with the vocabulary word missing from the center. This can be used as an assessment as students determine the missing word based upon the evidence included in the Frayer. A Concept Card has basically the same framework as a Frayer, with four corners and the term on the back, but students do not have to include examples and non-examples as specific to a Frayer. These can be used by students as flash cards in centers, learning stations, or individually for review.

Having students reflect on their work, being metacognitive, is one of the simplest ways to implement authentic opportunities for writing in most classes. Students can reflect on what they did (the activity or task itself), why they did it, and the value they found in doing it. In a Journey's Notebook, the primary purpose of the output page is to have students reflect on the work they did on the input page. Students can analyze errors that they made or others made, explain the strategies they used, and clarify why those strategies were chosen. There are several reflections that are used throughout the book (see Table 2.1).

Table 2.1 Reflection Matrix

Location	Activity	Reflection Tool	Figure
Chapter 3	Puzzling Problems Task Cards	QUAD Reflection	See page 86
Chapter 4	Matching Mania/Grid Games	Checking in Reflection	See page 114
Chapter 4	ABC Sum Race	ABC Sum Race Reflection	See page 115
Chapter 4	Multiple Representation Match	MRM Pentagon Reflection	See page 116
Chapter 4	Visual Vocabulary	Visual Vocabulary Reflection (R.A.F.T.)	See page 117

Making meaning, inquiry, and creating ideas are three related opportunities for writing. Students benefit from having opportunities to first make meaning. Making meaning can easily be facilitated by using visuals. Using a picture or visual prompt increases accessibility to more students because reading is no longer a stumbling block. Students simply think about what they see. Some questions that might be used to prompt students as they are thinking include:

◆ What types of questions do I have about what I see?
◆ What types of questions might need to be asked or answered about what I see?

Students are making meaning on their own before we guide them to the more focused path we want them to explore. Too often educators think they must give meaning to students; we don't develop the skill sets that allow students to take some risks to make meaning on their own. Using visuals allows students to take risks; it allows teachers to take what students say, build some structure around their comments, offer language for the ideas, and provide scaffolding to lead them to desired conclusions. Once students begin to make meaning, they have more questions, which lead to creating ideas.

Providing time and opportunity for students to make meaning
vs.
initially giving students meaning

Using a visual prompt may put the teacher into a risk-taking situation. Student responses may not be anticipated and teachers may feel that they are not prepared for any response, idea, or question that arises as students make meaning, ask questions, and create ideas. Traditionally, social studies and ELA teachers have struggled less with this than the more analytical fields of mathematics and science. Free writing and journal prompts lend themselves to being used when students are making meaning. A **Think-WRITE-Pair-Share** is an opportunity for students to think and write BEFORE they pair with a peer and share their thoughts (Figure 2.3). This way students are responsible for capturing their own thoughts initially. If students just think, pair, and then share, others' thoughts sometimes become their own because they agree with their peers or think others' ideas sound better.

The Think-WRITE-Pair-Share as an initial open writing gives way to writing in a more focused manner. Teachers can provide informational text sources for the students to use as primary sources as they work through the questions they have. Sources can be chosen that lead students on the journey the teacher seeks without the teacher having to lead every step of the way. From there, more extended writing can occur as students create products and educate others to report their findings or conclusions. Students are following the basic writing process of generating ideas, developing and organizing thoughts, and then revising and editing their work. Again, traditionally ELA and social studies teachers had more experience using the writing process than those in mathematics, science, and other disciplines. Revising and editing connect directly back to showing evidence and reflecting on their work.

Figure 2.3 Think-WRITE-Pair-Share. A reproducible version of this tool is available in Appendix B (p. 120).

Think-WRITE-Pair-Share

Think about . . .

WRITE about what questions come to mind in the area below.

PAIR with your partner and discuss what each of you wrote.

Be prepared to SHARE with the whole group.

If students have not been doing a lot of writing previously in a non-ELA classroom, it may be difficult to get students to do extended writing as they are making meaning. To build stamina in students for their writing, students need to have opportunities with open writing that then move to more focused writing, and finally, to more extended writing (see Figure 2.4).

The last two opportunities for students to engage with writing are through educating, which is often linked to producing a product. Students educate with writing based upon the purpose for the writing. Is the writing to

Figure 2.4 Writing Opportunities

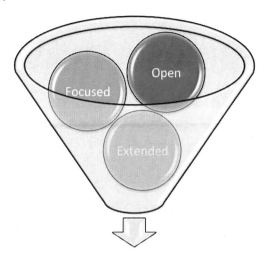

Writing Opportunities

persuade, is it to describe, or is it simply a narrative? These are questions that students must think about as they are writing to educate. The International Reading Association, along with the National Council of Teachers of English, have a wonderful website, ReadWriteThink (www.readwritethink.org), where there are many resources for teachers of all subjects (not just ELA). There are classroom interactives that can be used by students as they are producing that are especially helpful for younger students or students who are challenged by technology.

Check out all of the sample tasks for sample journal prompts provided, as well as ideas for using vocabulary and writing. Adapt them to your particular content or topic.

For all of the sample tasks, a sample journal prompt is provided along with ideas for using vocabulary and writing. One favorite strategy is the R.A.F.T.: students assume a **R**ole to use as their voice as they talk to a specific **A**udience using a prescribed **F**ormat for a content **T**opic (Figure 2.5). A sample, the Visual Vocabulary Reflection, can be found in Appendix B (on p. 117).

Figure 2.5 R.A.F.T. Writing Strategy

If you need a fresh approach to integrating a notebook into your class-room, using a Journey's Notebook can change the way you teach as well as how your students learn and experience their content. "The notebook becomes a dynamic place where language, data, and logical reasoning experiences operate jointly to form meaning for the student" (Jones). A Journey's Notebook helps students create an organized space for demonstrating their learning process. The notebook serves as a formative instructional tool as well as a portfolio of the students' learning experiences that provides rich documentation for their logical reasoning development. It is a tangible representation of the content practices, and it serves as a platform for turning conjecture into modeling and STEM and STEAM curriculum integrations.

Writing is one of the parts of language that students are still developing at every grade level. What some students (ESL/ELL, for example) know about content may exceed their ability to communicate it through the written word. For that reason, students can use pictures and diagrams to support their efforts to communicate their experiences.

Students learn to write by writing, and their writing needs to develop original thought, not just copy something that someone else wrote. Therefore, teachers must provide opportunities for students to engage in writing about the content they are investigating and cultivate an environment that is rich in content-specific language. Providing students with a Journey's Notebook, if for nothing other than the development of a Glossary and a Journal, offers students a place where they can record their thoughts and experiences to chronicle their growth over time while on their educational journey. Students' writing should include discussions about what they did, how they thought—and why they thought or did what they did—and it should use correct academic language. Students' writing should make sense and be complete. This will develop over time for students as they have more opportunities to write about their experiences.

Two of the main components of a Journey's Notebook are the Glossary and the Journal. In developing a Glossary, as stated previously, students write down their initial thoughts about terms and vocabulary words. *IDK* is not allowed. Through effective discourse and debriefing, students' knowledge and understanding can be pre-assessed. Students annotate their writing—they do not erase—as they correct misconceptions and add to their knowledge and understanding. Having vocabulary strategies is also vital as students build fluency in every discipline. The Vocabulary Ribbon offers a strategy for a flexible cumulative vocabulary review. (A reproducible version of this tool is available in Appendix B on p. 119.) Students combine work with vocabulary and writing as they engage with Compare and Contrast, which has students writing summary sentences about word pairs.

Journal prompts can involve quotes, historical connections to topics, famous people related to the topic of study, misconceptions, and "What if?" scenarios. This is merely the beginning of ideas for using the Journal. When using quotes from famous content-related people, famous historical people, or current events, ask the students to write the quote and then write briefly about what they think the quoted person meant in light of their time period and circumstances. Students can also be asked to write about how the quote has meaning for them in this particular class or discipline or in their lives. Math-ographies, Hist-ographies, Science-ographies, etc. can be prompted early in the year so students can share their past experiences with the disciplines as well as their projections for how knowledge of that field will impact their future.

Writing About is a small-group writing activity that connects a topic's vocabulary to writing. This is a good activity for struggling students and ESL/ELL who need some support when writing. Give students two or three index cards or scraps of paper. Students study a word cloud for the topic and write one, two, or three sentences about the topic, using words that they find in the word cloud. Students then share their individual sentences in small groups, and each group creates a paragraph about the topic. The index cards allow students to sequence their sentences to build a thoughtful and complete paragraph. They combine similar sentences, check for an introduction and conclusion, add transition words, and so on. This provides an opportunity for students to practice building a paragraph about the topic. This activity can be extended later as an individual writing activity in the Journey's Notebook. Note: Invite the ELA teacher to visit the class and share what makes a good paragraph so common expectations can be set that support the work in ELA as well as with the content.

There are many other features that can be included in a Journey's Notebook. Having students show their work, collect data, or take notes on an input page while capturing their thinking on an output page provides an automatic opportunity for students to reflect on each part of their topical study. For more information on using a notebook in the classroom, see the website for TLJ Consulting Group (http://tljconsultinggroup.com/).

3

The Journey to Deeper Understandings: Building Practices

A Structure for Developing Deeper Understanding Through Logical Reasoning

> Memorizing formulas is no more mathematics than memorizing dates is history or memorizing spelling words is literature.[1]
>
> (Rusczyk)

Today's college and career readiness standards require teachers at all levels to provide authentic contextual experiences regularly for their students. At all levels, students are challenged when engaging in contextually based scenarios that go beyond the basic procedure. Also, many teachers struggle knowing what strategies to incorporate that move the learner and the learning forward. Teachers often do not have the tools necessary to help students make sense of these more rigorous experiences. This section focuses on tools that address the following three challenges:

1. Students' lack of the skills needed to engage successfully in a rigorous contextual scenario.
2. Teachers' challenges with supporting the development of these skills through the use of effective differentiated questioning.
3. Students' heavy dependence upon facilitated guidance throughout the logical reasoning process.

Logical reasoning has traditionally been a challenge for many students, whether in the primary grades or high school. Knowing "how to teach" logical reasoning can be an equal challenge for the teacher. One of the difficulties when facilitating logical reasoning lies in the variety of situations that students encounter as well as the multiple strategies that can be applied to resolving them. Another obstacle facing teachers and students is the reading required for "making sense of problems." For some students, reading is the first roadblock in finding that "entry point" to engage in the situation.

The structure for effectively developing logical reasoning to ensure deeper understandings with rigorous content has three components (Figure 3.1). The first, the Logical Reasoning Process (LRP), involves the three phases students work through when engaging in logical reasoning. The associated support structures and scaffolds compose the second component. Third is

Figure 3.1 Three Phases of the Logical Reasoning Process

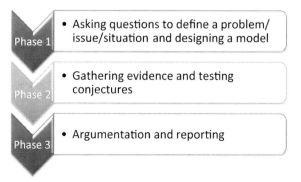

Phase 1
• Asking questions to define a problem/issue/situation and designing a model

Phase 2
• Gathering evidence and testing conjectures

Phase 3
• Argumentation and reporting

the accountability check: what to look for as students engage in logical reasoning and teachers are facilitating the experiences.

The Three Phases of the Logical Reasoning Process begin with Phase 1: through asking questions, students define an issue, a situation, a scenario, or a problem. From there, they design a model and/or develop a strategy with which to begin their reasoning process. In Phase 2, they use this model and/or these strategies to gather evidence and test possible conjectures. This cycle is not linear. When students begin their work and see the evidence they are gathering is not supporting their original plan, they adjust, refine, and move forward. Phase 3 involves students developing a logical argument and reporting on their results (Figure 3.2).

Figure 3.2 Support Structures for Building Logical Reasoning

The support structures embody the practices that are inherent in the discipline as well as effective questioning, strategies, and activities that maximize student success. Various strategies and activities have been identified to engage students in the practices. Four opportunities for questioning have been identified to support the facilitation of the strategies/activities.

The Logical Reasoning Process: A Closer Look

The Logical Reasoning Process can be used to assist students in making sense of problems/issues as well as in decontextualizing and contextualizing given information.

> The process also requires students to construct viable arguments as they formulate their ideas about the meaning of the situation and make predictions about the outcome. Once they obtain a proposed solution, students compare it to the prediction to determine its reasonableness. Following explicit steps to unpack the problem/issue, students begin the process with minimal to no teacher guidance and complete the initial steps. This step eliminates the blank piece of paper or the famous "I don't know" answer. Using a consistent process over time will assist students in becoming more successful with logical reasoning. While this process may not always fit every problem/issue, it does help students develop a systematic approach to finding the entry point for tasks.
>
> (Texas and Jones, 2013)

To explicitly facilitate students successfully solving contextual problems/issues, teachers need to address several components. Students often struggle with reading and understanding (decoding) the text as well as employing a strategy for getting started. Having a structure for organizing one's thinking and fully answering the question that was posed (rather than responding with an initial solution/explanation) are other challenges students face. A graphic organizer that supports the development of logical reasoning is used to assist students in working independently.

Note that in several of the samples of student work, students created a graphic organizer by dividing a plain piece of paper into regions for their work. Using paper folding allows students to increase their work area by using legal paper or chart paper, etc., instead of just standard 8.5 × 11-inch paper.

The LRP Graphic Organizer (Figure 3.3) is a tool for students who need a supporting structure to help organize their work flow. It guides the process of logical reasoning. Once students have internalized this process, the graphic organizer is no longer needed. However, when new problem types, scenario types, and more complex issues are introduced, it may prove once again to be a helpful tool.

As they enter Phase I of the LRP, students first define the problem/issue given and restate it as an answer statement (possibly as a fill-in-the-blank statement). Step 1, in the bottom right-hand corner, is where students begin (and end) their work with the LRP and in this graphic organizer. Students continue to Step 2 on the organizer as they identify useful information for the task or problem. They then devise a plan, create a model, and/or determine strategies to use in Step 3.

As students are moving from Step 3 to Step 4, they transition into Phase II of the LRP. Once a model has been developed, and strategies selected, students begin working to gather evidence, conjecture, and test out their

Figure 3.3 Logical Reasoning Process Graphic Organizer. A reproducible version of this tool is available in Appendix A (p. 80).

ideas. In this step, students check their work, determine whether the strategy or model developed is reliable, and decide to continue or back up and refine and adjust their initial thoughts. The bulk of the students' work gets completed here; this is where connections are made.

As students begin Step 5, they revisit Step 1 by formalizing the answer statement. Phase III requires students to argue and report their findings. Here, students can be offered some flexibility in how they choose to report their findings and communicate the supporting argument. Figure 3.4 shows the three phases.

As students engage in the phases of the Logical Reasoning Process, they are also engaging in practices for the specific content with which they are working. The LRP is a method through which the skills and habits that make for successful students are developed. This is evidenced by the alignment of the practices from each of the content standards that are employed across the phases of the LRP.

Just as students in mathematics are making sense of problems, language arts students are demonstrating independence with their reading and comprehending. Students in all content areas are asking questions, defining

Figure 3.4 Logical Reasoning Process Graphic Organizer with Phases of the Logical Reasoning Process

problems, and reasoning as they begin their work in Phase 1. Defining the problem at hand, gathering information that is given as well as determining information that may be needed but not given, and beginning to develop a plan of attack are basic skills that all students need to build for today's more rigorous standards.

Phase 2 of the LRP embodies the bulk of the work of the students in all content areas. As students are working with their model or working through their plan, they are regularly testing and checking their work as well as gathering and checking the reliability of the evidence they are collecting. This information being gathered provides the basis for the work that will be done in Phase 3. It is in this phase that students must be cognizant of who their audience is and the purpose of the task.

All content disciplines incorporate practices specifically focused on reporting the conclusions reached through the work. Creating viable arguments with supporting evidence is required. Students are communicating their conclusions and, if needed, taking informed actions based upon the results of their work. These practices are some of the more rigorous of which students must show evidence on today's assessments (Figure 3.5).

Figure 3.5 Logical Reasoning Process Graphic Organizer with Content Practices

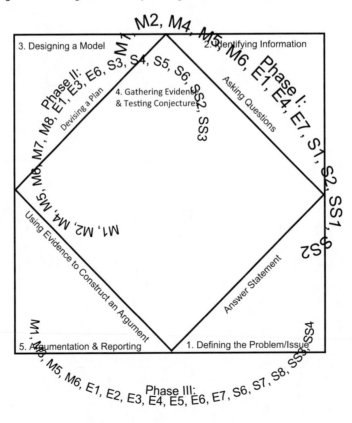

Standards for Mathematical Practice

M1: Make sense of problems and persevere in solving them.
M2: Reason abstractly and quantitatively.
M3: Construct viable arguments and critique the reasoning of others.
M4: Model with mathematics.
M5: Use appropriate tools strategically.
M6: Attend to precision.
M7: Look for and make use of structure.
M8: Look for and express regularity in repeated reasoning.

(Common Core State Standards Initiative, 2012, pp. 6–8)

English Language Arts Standards Student Portraits

E1: They demonstrate independence.
E2: They build strong content knowledge.
E3: They respond to the varying demands of audience, task, purpose, and discipline.
E4: They comprehend as well as critique.
E5: They value evidence.
E6: They use technology and digital media strategically and capably.
E7: They come to understand other perspectives and cultures.

(Common Core State Standards Initiative, 2010, p. 7)

Next Generation Science Standards Science and Engineering Practices

S1: Asking Questions and Defining Problems
S2: Developing and Using Models
S3: Planning and Carrying Out Investigations
S4: Analyzing and Interpreting Data
S5: Using Mathematics and Computational Thinking
S6: Constructing Explanations and Designing Solutions
S7: Engaging in Argument from Evidence
S8: Obtaining, Evaluating, and Communicating Information

(Next Generation Science Standards, 2013)

C3 Framework for Social Studies State Standards (Dimensions)

SS1: Developing Questions and Planning Inquiries
SS2: Applying Disciplinary Concepts and Tools
SS3: Evaluating Sources and Using Evidence
SS4: Communicating Conclusions and Taking Informed Action

(NCSS, 2013)

Full explanations for each of the disciplines' practice standards listed here are in Appendix D (p. 138).

Providing Support Structures and Opportunities for Effective Questioning for the LRP

Students for whom entering the conversation is challenging benefit from the teacher effectively questioning to move the learners and the learning forward. Four opportunities for questioning exist (Figure 3.6) that will support the learner and the learning. These opportunities can be incorporated into the LRP (Figure 3.7).

Entry: questions for students having difficulty getting started (Step 1 & Step 2)

Moving: questions for places where students could get stuck (Step 2, Step 3, & Step 4)

Reflection: questions for students to use for metacognition after completing the problem/issue (Step 4 & Step 5)

Extension: questions for students to engage in higher-order thinking skills with respect to the same concept and/or problem (after completing Step 5 & returning to Step 1)

There are a few basic questions that serve most logical reasoning scenarios that have been developed through years of teaching and consulting.

Figure 3.6 Four Opportunities for Questioning

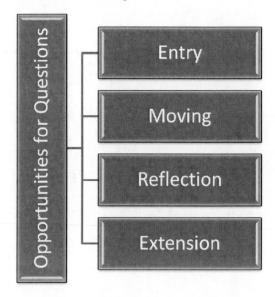

Figure 3.7 Logical Reasoning Process Graphic Organizer with the Opportunities for Questioning

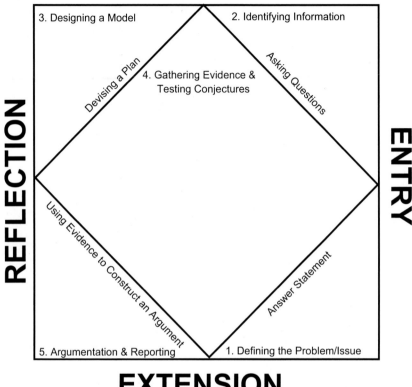

Questions beyond these should be refined to be task specific. Here is a sampling of questions that can be asked at each phase:

Entry: questions for students having difficulty getting started

- ◆ What is the problem asking?
- ◆ How might you identify from the text the problem, question, or dilemma?
- ◆ How can the scenario be restated as an answer statement?

Moving: questions for places where students could get stuck

- ◆ What information do you know?
- ◆ What additional information might be needed?
- ◆ What vocabulary or symbols need to be defined?

Reflection: questions for students to use for metacognition after completing problem

- ◆ What pattern(s) and/or relationship(s) exist?
- ◆ What types of evidence are needed to support this reasoning?
- ◆ How does this answer satisfy the question posed?

Extension: questions for students to engage in higher-order thinking skills with respect to the same concept and/or problem

- ◆ How would the solution change if the constraints in the situation were changed?
- ◆ Why did . . . ?
- ◆ How might you use the patterns/relationships you identified to make a general conjecture about . . . ?

A reproducible student version of the Opportunities for Questioning is in Appendix A (p. 83).

The entry questions (and possibly the moving questions) can be projected on the board to allow student groups access to these questions. Allow students to attempt the problem/issue for a brief period before offering these guiding questions as support. This think time will teach students to try to make sense of the problem/issue and not automatically look to the teacher for guidance. Too many students have learned that playing helpless is the best way to get the teacher to "tell them what to do." The role of the LRP is to support students working independently. Another approach would be to create "clue cards" by printing these clusters of questions on a strip of paper and placing them at the students' work area for reference. Make sure to tell students that these questions have been generated to help them help themselves by taking ownership of their learning and being resources for one another (Wiliam and Thompson, 2007).

The reflection questions and extension questions can also be made into "clue cards" and given to students as they move through the process. These are the questions that allow for differentiation for those students who complete the problem early and need to move deeper. For students who finish early, one possible extension is to help their peers. The following rules are suggested:

1. They are not allowed to use declarative sentences that "tell what to do."
2. They are not able to show their paper and what they did.
3. They are not able to take a pencil and write for the peer.
4. They are only allowed to ask the peer questions to assist them in their understanding. (They need to write down the questions that seemed to help move the learning forward.)

Connecting the Phases of Logical Reasoning with the Graphic Organizer

The Puzzling Problem strategy (Texas and Jones, 2013) helps make challenging content more accessible to all students. Providing the set-up through puzzle pieces offers a nonthreatening environment for students to work with more challenging content. Puzzle pieces can be differentiated to support diverse learners as well as create pairs for collaborative learning. The directions are as follows:

1. Enlarge a task to fit on one sheet of card stock. Cut the task into puzzle pieces. The number of pieces can correspond to the number of students per group, or you can give each student multiple pieces of the same puzzle.
2. Give each student a puzzle piece or pieces.
3. Students must match their puzzle pieces to form a task to consider.
4. As a learning group, students select a strategy to address the problem/issue.
5. Students resolve the issue as a team and submit a proposal. The team must be able to construct a viable argument for their solution and document it individually as a journal activity.

See Appendix A (p. 84) for detailed facilitation notes for the Puzzling Problems activity.

Sample Tasks

Table 3.1 Opportunities for Writing Task Alignment (High School)*

Subjects	Task	Visual Vocabulary	Frayer Model/ Graphic Organizer	Compare & Contrast	Writing About	Vocabulary Ribbon	Showing Evidence	Reflecting	Creating Ideas	Inquiry	Making Meaning	Educating	Producing Products	Journey's Notebook
Math	Apples in a Bowl		X		X			QUAD	Logical Reasoning Process: Steps 1–3			X	X	X
Science Math CTE	Hot Air Cold Body©—TI	Specific to unit of study		X		Can be used at any time	X	QUAD	Logical Reasoning Process: Steps 1–3				X	X
SS ELA Math	Stories from the Past			X	X			QUAD	Logical Reasoning Process: Steps 1–3			X	X	X
CTE SS ELA	Wind Energy		X				X	QUAD	Logical Reasoning Process: Steps 1–3				X	X
		Vocabulary					**Writing Opportunities**							

*Matrices are located in Appendix B (pp. 103–106) to illustrate the progression and development of topics across K–12.

Apples in a Bowl

Applicable Subject Areas: Mathematics

Apples in a Bowl is an adaptation of a classic problem involving unit fractions with consecutive whole number denominators. This task at the secondary level provides the opportunity for students to review their understanding of fractions as they connect working with fractions to writing a single equation as a model for the task.

One night, Father Jones couldn't sleep, so he went down into the kitchen, where he found a bowl full of apples. Being hungry, he took 1/6 of the apples.

Later that same night, Mother Jones was hungry and couldn't sleep. She, too, found the apples and took 1/5 of what Father Jones had left.

Still later, Baylan, the oldest Jones son, awoke, went to the kitchen, and ate 1/4 of the remaining apples.

Even later, his brother, Eson, ate 1/3 of what was then left.

Finally, the third son, Kensen, ate 1/2 of what was left, leaving only three apples for Grandmother Jones to use to make a pie.

How many apples were originally in the bowl?

Figure 3.8 Apples in a Bowl Puzzling Problem

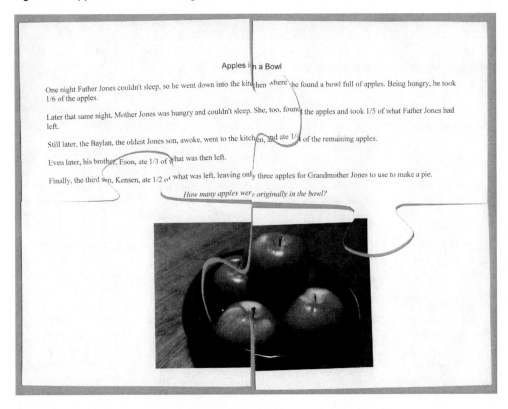

Apples in a Bowl

One night Father Jones couldn't sleep, so he went down into the kitchen where he found a bowl full of apples. Being hungry, he took 1/6 of the apples.

Later that same night, Mother Jones was hungry and couldn't sleep. She, too, found the apples and took 1/5 of what Father Jones had left.

Still later, the Baylan, the oldest Jones son, awoke, went to the kitchen, and ate 1/4 of the remaining apples.

Even later, his brother, Eson, ate 1/3 of what was then left.

Finally, the third son, Kensen, ate 1/2 of what was left, leaving only three apples for Grandmother Jones to use to make a pie.

How many apples were originally in the bowl?

Figure 3.9 Sample Completed Logical Reasoning Process Graphic Organizer

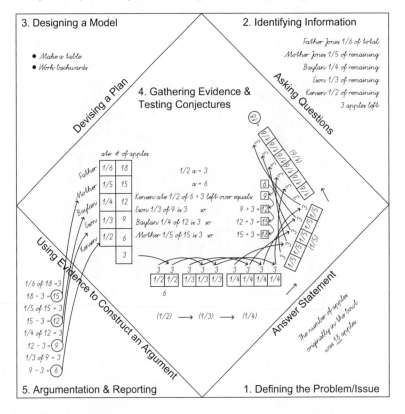

Figure 3.10 Apples in a Bowl. The task card and these task-specific questions are available in Appendix A (pp. 88–89).

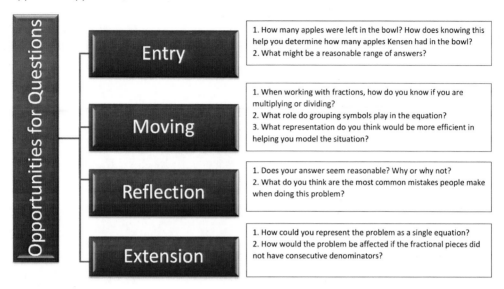

Opportunities for Questions

Entry
1. How many apples were left in the bowl? How does knowing this help you determine how many apples Kensen had in the bowl?
2. What might be a reasonable range of answers?

Moving
1. When working with fractions, how do you know if you are multiplying or dividing?
2. What role do grouping symbols play in the equation?
3. What representation do you think would be more efficient in helping you model the situation?

Reflection
1. Does your answer seem reasonable? Why or why not?
2. What do you think are the most common mistakes people make when doing this problem?

Extension
1. How could you represent the problem as a single equation?
2. How would the problem be affected if the fractional pieces did not have consecutive denominators?

Suggested Trade Books

Fraction Fun by David Adler

Funny and Fabulous Fraction Stories by Dan Greenberg

The Wishing Club by Donna Jo Napoli

Secrets, Lies, and Algebra by Wendy Lichtman

Making Meaning and Creating Ideas

An inherent writing opportunity exists for students as they begin to work on the task using the LRP. For example, teachers can get the students started by employing the Think-WRITE-Pair-Share strategy, incorporating the first three steps of the LRP. Once they have determined a strategy, students may then partner and share in their work as they complete the LRP. Students are also inquiring as they ask questions that may need to be answered as they work through the task.

Reflecting and Inquiry

Students can use the QUAD Reflection for Puzzling Problems once they have completed the task. (See p. 86 in Appendix A for a black line master of the QUAD reflection.)

Vocabulary

Frayer Model: Equation

Writing About: Equations

A reproducible version of the vocabulary and writing ideas for this task is available in Appendix B (pp. 107–108).

Educating and Producing Products

Students create a Press Release on the benefits and limitations of at least three different strategies that can be employed in working with the task. The Press Release will be shared with middle school students as a resource as they are building their problem-solving toolkit.

Journey's Notebook Journal

"I don't care much for equations myself. This is partly because it is difficult for me to write them down, but mainly because I don't have an intuitive feeling for equations." —Stephen Hawking

> See Chapter 2 for facilitation ideas on using quotes with students in the Journal section of the Journey's Notebook.

Hot Air, Cold Body: Using Newton's Law of Cooling to Determine Time of Death[2]

Applicable Subject Areas: Science, Mathematics, and CTE

High school physics students, acting as Forensic Scientists, are to determine the time of death of the crime victim. Given the scenario shown below with the information obtained from the crime scene, students must create a lab model to determine the coefficient of cooling. This activity suggests using potatoes as "bodies," and the experiment is set up with guided facilitation in the teacher notes provided by Texas Instruments. Newton's Law of Cooling will be employed. This activity is used with permission by Texas Instruments, Inc. The TI-Nspire Activity Files, Student Worksheets, and Teacher Notes can be downloaded from: https://education.ti.com/en/tisciencenspired/us/forensics/case-files.

Use Newton's law of cooling to narrow down the number of suspects by determining when the victim was killed.

Memo to Detective Sergeant

The elevator operator of the Ritz Palace Hotel died from a stab wound while on duty last Thursday evening. His body was discovered by a family on its way down to the pool. When we arrived at the scene, we canvassed the area but found nothing. The elevator is full of fingerprints of the hundreds of guests who ride it during the day. We have several suspects in mind, but we are having trouble pinning down the time of death. If we can determine that, we have a good shot at finding the killer.

Enclosed are a photograph of the crime scene and part of the paramedic report.

Paramedic report
Date: 10/5/05
Time: 9:45 p.m.
Body temperature: 29.0°C
Notes: Elevator temperature was high; thermostat set at 27°C.

Figure 3.11 Hot Air, Cold Body Puzzling Problem

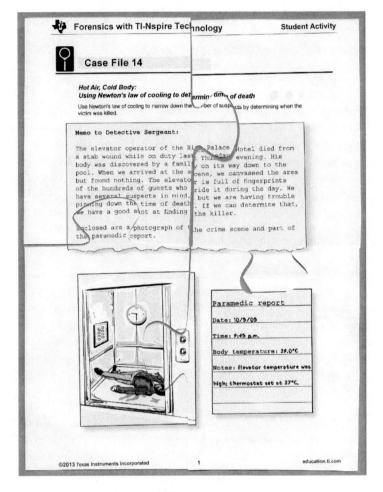

Case File 14

Hot Air, Cold Body:
Using Newton's law of cooling to determine time of death

Use Newton's law of cooling to narrow down the number of suspects by determining when the victim was killed.

Memo to Detective Sergeant:

The elevator operator of the Ritz Palace Hotel died from a stab wound while on duty last Thursday evening. His body was discovered by a family on its way down to the pool. When we arrived at the scene, we canvassed the area but found nothing. The elevator is full of fingerprints of the hundreds of guests who ride it during the day. We have several suspects in mind, but we are having trouble pinning down the time of death. If we can determine that, we have a good shot at finding the killer.

Enclosed are a photograph of the crime scene and part of the paramedic report.

Paramedic report

Date: 10/5/05

Time: 9:45 p.m.

Body temperature: 29.0°C

Notes: Elevator temperature was high; thermostat set at 27°C.

Figure 3.12 Hot Air, Cold Body Sample Completed LRP Graphic Organizer

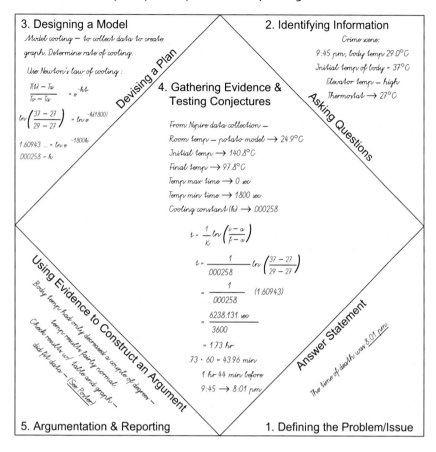

3. Designing a Model
Model cooling — to collect data to create graph. Determine rate of cooling.

Use Newton's law of cooling :

$$\frac{T(t) - T_a}{T_o - T_a} = e^{-kt}$$

$$ln\left(\frac{37 - 27}{29 - 27}\right) = ln\,e^{-k(1800)}$$

$$1.60943\ldots = ln\,e^{-1800k}$$

$$.000258 = k$$

Devising a Plan

2. Identifying Information
Crime scene:
9:45 pm, body temp 29.0°C
Initial temp of body = 37°C
Elevator temp — high
Thermostat → 27°C

Asking Questions

4. Gathering Evidence & Testing Conjectures

From Nspire data collection —
Room temp — potato model → 24.9°C
Initial temp → 140.8°C
Final temp → 97.8°C
Temp max time → 0 sec
Temp min time → 1800 sec
Cooling constant (k) → .000258

$$t = \frac{1}{k}\,ln\left(\frac{v - \alpha}{t - \alpha}\right)$$

$$t = \frac{1}{.000258}\,ln\left(\frac{37 - 27}{29 - 27}\right)$$

$$= \frac{1}{.000258}\,(1.60943)$$

$$= \frac{6238.131\;sec}{3600}$$

$$= 1.73\;hr$$

$$.73 \cdot 60 = 43.96\;min$$

1 hr 44 min before
9:45 → 8:01 pm

Using Evidence to Construct an Argument
Body temp had only decreased a couple of degrees —
temp results fairly normal.
Check results w/ table and graph —
did fit data — (See Poster)

Answer Statement
The time of death was 8:01 pm.

5. Argumentation & Reporting

1. Defining the Problem/Issue

Figure 3.13 Hot Air, Cold Body. The task card and these task-specific questions are available in Appendix A (pp. 90–91).

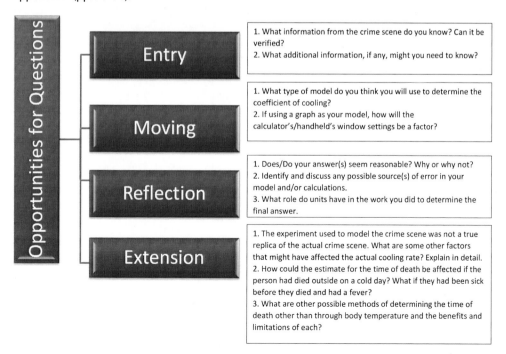

Opportunities for Questions

Entry
1. What information from the crime scene do you know? Can it be verified?
2. What additional information, if any, might you need to know?

Moving
1. What type of model do you think you will use to determine the coefficient of cooling?
2. If using a graph as your model, how will the calculator's/handheld's window settings be a factor?

Reflection
1. Does/Do your answer(s) seem reasonable? Why or why not?
2. Identify and discuss any possible source(s) of error in your model and/or calculations.
3. What role do units have in the work you did to determine the final answer.

Extension
1. The experiment used to model the crime scene was not a true replica of the actual crime scene. What are some other factors that might have affected the actual cooling rate? Explain in detail.
2. How could the estimate for the time of death be affected if the person had died outside on a cold day? What if they had been sick before they died and had a fever?
3. What are other possible methods of determining the time of death other than through body temperature and the benefits and limitations of each?

Suggested Trade Books

The Mysteries of Beethoven's Hair by Russell Martin and Lydia Nibley

Written in Bone: Buried Lives of Jamestown and Colonial Maryland by Sally M. Walker

CSI Expert!: Forensic Science for Kids by Karen Schultz

Science Sleuths: Solving Mysteries Using Scientific Investigations by Howard Schindler

Stiff: The Curious Lives of Human Cadavers by Mary Roach

Making Meaning and Creating Ideas

An inherent writing opportunity exists for students as they begin to work on the task using the LRP. For example, teachers can get the students started by employing the Think-Write-Pair-Share strategy, incorporating the first three steps of the LRP. Once they have determined a strategy, students may then partner and share in their work as they complete the LRP. Students are also inquiring as they ask questions that may need to be answered as they work through the task.

Reflecting and Inquiry

Students can use the QUAD Reflection for Puzzling Problems once they have completed the task. (See p. 86 in Appendix A for a black line master of the QUAD reflection.)

Vocabulary

Compare & Contrast: Hot Air, Cold Body

A reproducible version of the vocabulary and writing ideas for this task is available in Appendix B (p. 110).

Producing Products and Showing Evidence

Poster Project: report out findings while showing evidence of the validity of the work done.

Journey's Notebook Journal

Describe the evidence used in the work today as well as the methods used in determining the time of death. Compare to how the process would have looked 50 years ago and 100 years ago.

Stories from the Past: World Heritage Sites

Applicable Subject Areas: Social Studies, ELA, and Mathematics

The UNESCO World Heritage Sites offer students an engaging environment in which to study both the concepts of nature conservation and the preservation of cultural properties. This activity provides an opportunity for collaboration between teachers of several disciplines—even mathematics—as students create a scale model. For the sake of this example, the LRP used for brainstorming the beginning development of the scale model part of the task is shown.

According to UNESCO, "The idea of creating an international movement for protecting heritage emerged after World War I. The 1972 Convention concerning the Protection of the World Cultural and Natural Heritage developed from the merging of two separate movements: the first focusing on the preservation of cultural sites, and the other dealing with the conservation of nature."[3]

Research the Strategic Objectives—the "Five Cs" of the World Heritage Convention. Prepare a presentation reporting your findings.

Create a "Top 10" list of World Heritage Sites. Validate the reasoning behind your "Top 10" list, being sure to cite primary sources. Include a map showing the locations for your "Top 10" list picks. Create a scale model of your top-pick site using an appropriate scale. Include the "Story from the Past" about your top pick.

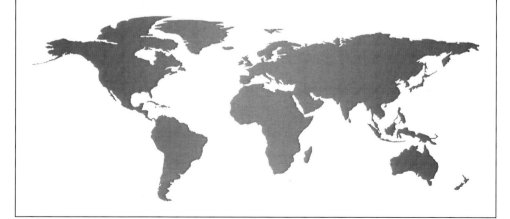

Figure 3.14 Stories from the Past Puzzling Problem

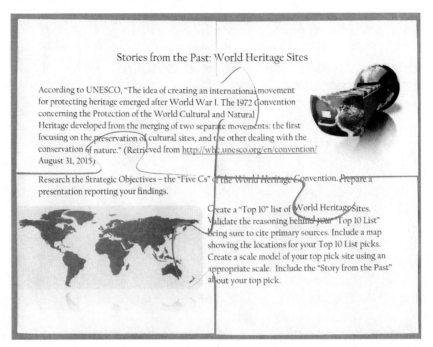

Figure 3.15 Stories from the Past Sample Completed LRP Graphic Organizer

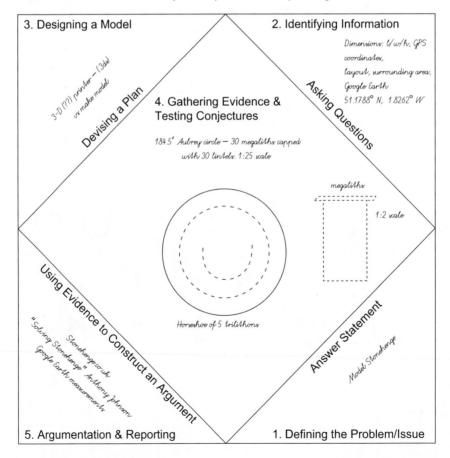

Other aspects for which the LRP might be used include the Five Cs, the Strategic Objectives of the World Heritage Convention, a plan for determining the Top 10 sites, etc.

Figure 3.16 Stories from the Past. The task card and these task-specific questions are available in Appendix A (pp. 92–93).

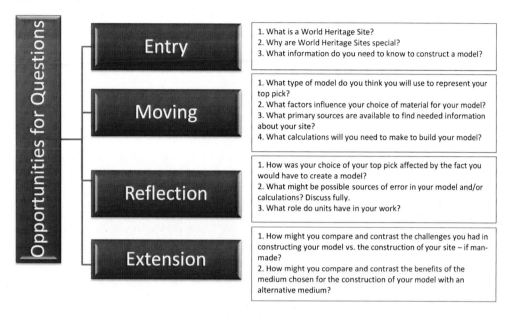

Opportunities for Questions

Entry
1. What is a World Heritage Site?
2. Why are World Heritage Sites special?
3. What information do you need to know to construct a model?

Moving
1. What type of model do you think you will use to represent your top pick?
2. What factors influence your choice of material for your model?
3. What primary sources are available to find needed information about your site?
4. What calculations will you need to make to build your model?

Reflection
1. How was your choice of your top pick affected by the fact you would have to create a model?
2. What might be possible sources of error in your model and/or calculations? Discuss fully.
3. What role do units have in your work?

Extension
1. How might you compare and contrast the challenges you had in constructing your model vs. the construction of your site – if man-made?
2. How might you compare and contrast the benefits of the medium chosen for the construction of your model with an alternative medium?

Suggested Trade Books

World Heritage Sites by UNESCO

Journeys of a Lifetime by National Geographic

Managing World Heritage Sites by Anna Leask and Alan Fyall

Stonehenge a New Understanding: Solving the Mysteries of the Greatest Stone Age Monument by Mike Parker Pearson

Solving Stonehenge: The Key to an Ancient Enigma by Anthony Johnson

Making Meaning and Creating Ideas

An inherent writing opportunity exists for students as they begin to work on the task using the LRP. For example, teachers can get the students started by employing the Think-Write-Pair-Share strategy, incorporating the first three steps of the LRP. Once they have determined a strategy, students may then partner and share in their work as they complete the LRP. Students are also inquiring as they ask questions that may need to be answered as they work through the task.

Reflecting and Inquiry

Students can use the QUAD Reflection for Puzzling Problems once they have completed the task. (See p. 86 in Appendix A for a black line master of the QUAD reflection.)

Vocabulary

Compare & Contrast: Stories from the Past

Writing About: World Heritage Sites

A reproducible version of these vocabulary and writing ideas for this task is available in Appendix B (pp. 111–112).

Producing Products and Showing Evidence

Multimedia: Create a traveling display of models and other supporting artifacts that could be used to educate others at various places in the community, such as the local library.

Journey's Notebook Journal

For a brief discussion about a R.A.F.T., see page 13.

R.A.F.T.:

Role: Docent of the site

Audience: Visitors to the site

Format: Script

Topic: How this site qualified as a World Heritage Site: the three criteria

Wind Energy: Pros and Cons

Applicable Subject Areas: CTE, Social Studies, and ELA

Secondary students are charged with advising their community on the potential development of a wind farm. This task can be the basis of a more extensive project because it meets the criteria of an effective project, known as the 6As of Project-Based Learning (PBL): Authenticity, Academic Rigor, Applied Learning, Active Exploration, Adult Relationships, and Assessment Practices. It is not the purpose of this section to explore the details of PBL, but rather suggest how this task could be expanded. Here, the LRP tool can used to help students organize their thinking throughout various stages of the project process.

You are the Agricultural Extension Agent for your local district. You have had several calls from local farmers and landowners about the potential development of a wind farm by WindCo in your area. The citizens have asked you to help advise them on this matter. There is a community 4-H meeting next week. You need to do a brief survey of the pros and cons of wind energy and be able to summarize your findings in a presentation at the next community 4-H meeting so the district can make an educated choice.

Figure 3.17 Wind Energy Puzzling Problem

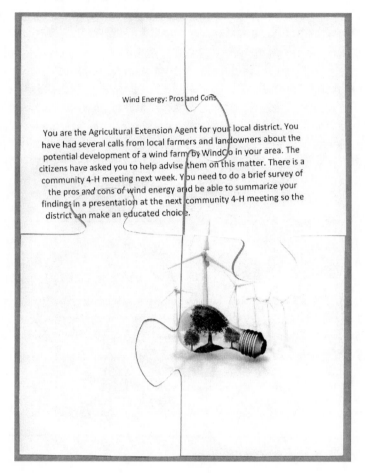

Figure 3.18 Wind Energy Sample Completed LRP Graphic Organizer

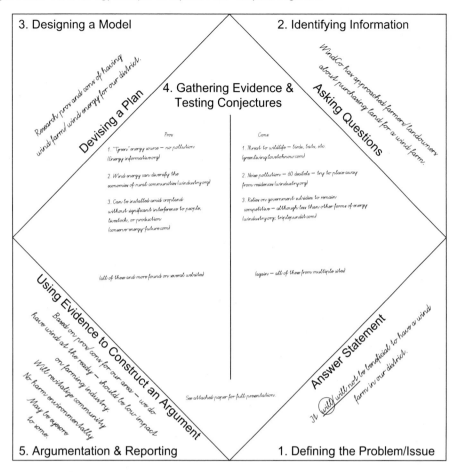

3. Designing a Model

2. Identifying Information

Research pros and cons of having wind farm/ wind energy for our district.

Devising a Plan

WindCo has approached farmers/landowners about purchasing land for a wind farm.

Asking Questions

4. Gathering Evidence & Testing Conjectures

Pros

1. "Green" energy source – no pollution (Energy informative.org)

2. Wind energy can diversify the economies of rural communities (windindustry.org)

3. Can be installed amid cropland without significant interference to people, livestock, or production (conserve-energy-future.com)

(all of these and more found on several websites)

Cons

1. Threat to wildlife – birds, bats, etc. (greenliving.lovetoknow.com)

2. Noise pollution – 80 decibels – try to place away from residence (windindustry.org)

3. Relies on government subsidies to remain competitive – although less than other forms of energy (windindustry.org; triplepundit.com)

(again – all of these from multiple sites)

See attached paper for full presentation.

Using Evidence to Construct an Argument

Based on pros/cons for our area – we do have wind at the ready – should be low impact on farming industry. Will revitalize community. No harm environmentally. May be eyesore to some.

Answer Statement

It will/will not be beneficial to have a wind farm in our district.

5. Argumentation & Reporting

1. Defining the Problem/Issue

Figure 3.19 Wind Energy. The task card and these task-specific questions are available in Appendix A (pp. 94–95).

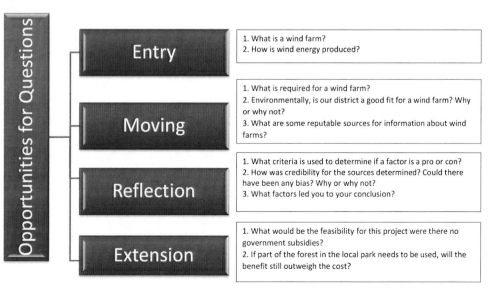

Opportunities for Questions

Entry
1. What is a wind farm?
2. How is wind energy produced?

Moving
1. What is required for a wind farm?
2. Environmentally, is our district a good fit for a wind farm? Why or why not?
3. What are some reputable sources for information about wind farms?

Reflection
1. What criteria is used to determine if a factor is a pro or con?
2. How was credibility for the sources determined? Could there have been any bias? Why or why not?
3. What factors led you to your conclusion?

Extension
1. What would be the feasibility for this project were there no government subsidies?
2. If part of the forest in the local park needs to be used, will the benefit still outweigh the cost?

Suggested Trade Books

Generating Wind Power by Niki Walker

Power from the Wind by Dan Chiras and Mick Sagrillo

Wind Energy Basics by Paul Gipe

Wind Power: The Struggle for Control of a New Global Industry by Ben Blackwell

Making Meaning and Creating Ideas

An inherent writing opportunity exists for students as they begin to work on the task using the LRP. For example, teachers can get the students started by employing the Think-Write-Pair-Share strategy, incorporating the first three steps of the LRP. Once they have determined a strategy, students may then partner and share in their work as they complete the LRP. Students are also inquiring as they ask questions that may need to be answered as they work through the task.

Reflecting and Inquiry

Students can use the QUAD Reflection for Puzzling Problems once they have completed the task. (See p. 86 in Appendix A for a black line master of the QUAD reflection.)

Vocabulary

Frayer Model: Renewable Energy

A reproducible version of this vocabulary task is available in Appendix B (p. 113).

Showing Evidence

Create an effective data display illustrating the results of the findings of the survey of the pros and cons of wind farms.

Producing Products

Prepare a slide presentation with an accompanying supporting pamphlet that includes the data display and cites the primary sources and evidence of the pros and cons found. Enough information needs to be shared to provide the citizens with the needed background to make an informed decision.

Journey's Notebook Journal

Draft a Public Service Announcement for the local media outlets to air to inform citizens who were unable to attend the 4-H meeting of what was discussed.

Growing Students' Capacity to Engage in Problem-Solving/Logical Reasoning

Give students the copy of "Opportunities for Questioning" Student Version and explain that good thinkers/problem-solvers ask themselves questions when facing a problem/scenario/dilemma. Have them put this in their notebook so they can refer to it anytime they are faced with a challenging task. This is also best used in conjunction with the LRP.

Begin with a task that you do not want students to fully solve but simply to work through the first two to three sections of the LRP. This will help build capacity for thinking through a scenario (versus focusing on solving a problem/issue/dilemma). This process includes determining what the task is asking, identifying important information, and considering a plan for addressing the problem/issue/dilemma.

Note: One possibility is to coordinate with an ELA teacher to do this part since it focuses on decoding informational text and translating questions into written answer statements. Students would then bring the pre-work to class. In order to assess whether or not all pertinent information has been gleaned from the problem, students would not be given the original problem again; instead, they would rely on the pre-work to propose a solution.

If students need assistance during the process, provide task-specific moving questions (Figure 3.20) as feedback to move them forward. In addition, reflection and extension questions can be used as they complete step 4 and move into step 5 and beyond.

As a reflection on the process, teachers can have students compare the general questioning tool and the task-specific set of questions to understand how the specific questions were generated. Students can begin to see patterns

Figure 3.20 Opportunities for Questioning Student Version. A reproducible version of this for students is in Appendix A (p. 83).

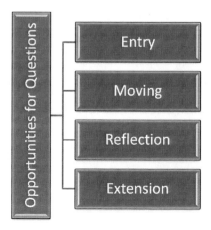

and understand the idea behind the thought process that occurs during problem-solving/reasoning. This should be done anytime there is teacher-provided, task-specific feedback. Over time, students should begin to internalize the intent of the process.

Students can be asked to use the task-specific questions with their partner as they work. In the beginning, teachers would provide the task-specific feedback questions and ask students to use them as they are supporting each other. The goal is for students to help each other through questioning rather than one student telling another what or how to work. Over time, students can begin to add questions to the list as they generate them in discussion with their partner. One step further would be for the partner to initial any of the questions that were asked that were truly helpful in generating understanding. This would be good feedback to the questioner as well as a great resource for additional questions that could be asked for the task.

The Q-Pyramid

A powerful set of tools—the Q-Pyramid and Overlay—connect the four opportunities for questioning to the LRP graphic organizer. Students and teachers can use the Q-Pyramid (see Figure 3.21) to support moving the learning and

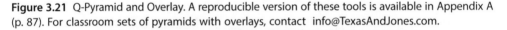

Figure 3.21 Q-Pyramid and Overlay. A reproducible version of these tools is available in Appendix A (p. 87). For classroom sets of pyramids with overlays, contact info@TexasAndJones.com.

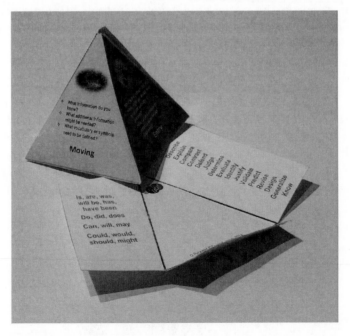

the learner forward whenever they engage in the Logical Reasoning Process. The Q-Pyramid is arranged with the LRP graphic organizer serving as the base of the pyramid while the faces correspond to the appropriate opportunities for questioning. The general set of questions for each of the four opportunities that exist within the work of the task is included on each face.

An Overlay is provided to facilitate creating task-specific questions. Question stems, verbs, and descriptors are provided. Teachers and students simply fill in the question with task-specific content. Teachers can use the Overlay to differentiate instruction through the deliberate and thoughtful preparation of questions, especially the reflection and extension ones. Students can use the Overlay to create their questions to help themselves move forward. Even the advanced student, who is often neglected, can now be challenged with authentic extensions instead of being punished by simply being given more things to do.

Using the "Apples in a Bowl" sample mathematics task, the following questions could be generated using the Overlay:

1. *How **can** you **determine*** the fractional part of the apples remaining in the bowl after each person eats a portion?
2. *What **are*** the factors that ***justify*** using the strategy you chose?

Using the "Wind Energy: Pros and Cons" sample interdisciplinary task, the following questions could be generated using the Overlay:

1. *Who **will*** benefit the most from the wind farm? The least? ***Describe*** how?
2. *What **could*** be some specific traits about our district that need to be considered in order to ***determine*** if the wind farm is a good idea?

> These stems were chosen to avoid questions that can be answered with a simple *yes* or *no*.

The question stems, verbs, and descriptors provided are simply an initial set to assist in developing the capacity to ask effective questions. They are by no means intended to be exhaustive lists. Words and phrases can be included between the stems, the verbs, and the descriptors to create a more fully developed question.

Most students who disengage do so because they do not know what to do, not because they don't care. These tools provide students with the support they need to help themselves and allow them to experience success while perfecting their logical reasoning skills. This beginning success will grow exponentially when nurtured. The goal is to have students be able to generate their own task-specific questions. Initially, they may have to use the general questions provided as a guide, but over time, even these will no longer be necessary.

Notes

1. Richard Rusczyk, retrieved from www.artofproblemsolving.com/articles/ what-is-problem-solving May 27, 2015.
2. © 2013 Texas Instruments Incorporated.
3. UNESCO, retrieved from http://whc.unesco.org/en/convention/ August 31, 2015.

Bibliography

Common Core State Standards Initiative. (2010). *Students Who Are College and Career Ready in Reading, Writing, Speaking, Listening, and Language.* Retrieved from www.corestandards.org/wp-content/uploads/ELA_Standards1.pdf

Common Core State Standards Initiative. (2012). *Standards for Mathematical Practice.* Retrieved from www.corestandards.org/wp-content/uploads/ Math_Standards.pdf

NCSS. (2013). *The College, Career, and Civic Life Framework.* Retrieved from www. socialstudies.org/system/files/c3/C3-Framework-for-Social-Studies.pdf

Next Generation Science Standards: For States, By States. (2013). Appendix F— Science and Engineering Practices in the NGSS. Retrieved from www. nextgenscience.org/sites/ngss/files/Appendix%20F%20%20Science%20 and%20Engineering%20Practices%20in%20the%20NGSS%20-%20 FINAL%20060513.pdf

Texas, L. A. and Jones, T. L. (2013). *Strategies for Common Core Mathematics: Implementing the Standards for Mathematical Practice 9–12.* New York: Routledge.

Wiliam, D. and Thompson, M. (2007). Integrating Assessment with Instruction: What Will It Take to Make It Work? In C. A. Dwyer (Ed.), *The Future of Assessment: Shaping Teaching and Learning* (pp. 53–82). Mahwah, NJ: Lawrence Erlbaum Associates.

4

The Journey from Practice to Proficiency: Strategies that Engage

Table 4.1 Strategies with Task Alignment: High School*

Subjects	Task	Matching Mania	Grid Games	ABC Sum Race	Vocabulary
Math	Apples in a Bowl				Vocabulary strategies are applicable to all subjects: **Visual Vocabulary, Vocabulary Ribbon, Reverse Frayer & Concept Card**
Science Math CTE	Hot Air, Cold Body©—TI			X	
SS ELA Math	Stories from the Past		X		
CTE SS ELA	Wind Energy	X			

*Matrices are located in Appendix C (pp. 121–122) to illustrate the progression and development of topics across K–12.

From Practice to Proficiency: An Overview

With today's more rigorous college and career readiness standards students are required to move beyond just acquisition of factual knowledge and development of basic procedural fluency. Developing conceptual understanding to a deeper level is the challenge for today's teachers and students. However,

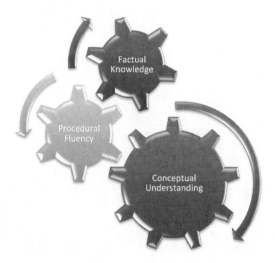

there is still a place and need for both factual knowledge and procedural fluency. Providing many diverse opportunities for students to experience engaging review allows students to develop fluencies and maintain their basic knowledge of key concepts.

The strategies offered in Chapter 4 can be used in small groups or learning stations once the strategies have been shared in the whole classroom setting. Then, further direct instruction can be focused on rich tasks and experiences that lead to students' deeper understanding of concepts being studied. For more mathematical examples of the first four strategies, see *Strategies for Common Core Mathematics: Implementing the Standards for Mathematical Practice K–5, 6–8, and 9–12* (Texas and Jones, 2013).

- ◆ **Matching Mania** is a strategy that incorporates a game to help students gain content knowledge in a nonthreatening environment. Students work cooperatively while practicing and strengthening their logical reasoning skills. **Checking In** is a traditional three-point reflection using squares, circles, and triangles that can be used with Matching Mania. Students can use it as a formative assessment tool to provide information on what they have mastered, what concepts they still have questions about, and implications for future learning.
- ◆ **Grid Games** is another strategy that incorporates a game to help students gain content knowledge in a nonthreatening environment. Students work cooperatively while practicing and strengthening their logical reasoning skills. **Checking In** is, as mentioned above, a three-point reflection using squares, circles, and triangles that can be used with Grid Games.
- ◆ **ABC Sum Race** is a strategy that uses reflective discussions and journaling as students engage in a competition to review conceptual knowledge and basic procedures. The **ABC Sum Race Reflection**

provides students with the opportunity to write about their thinking and their experiences in the activity.

◆ Several **vocabulary** strategies to support students' understanding of terms, symbols, and notations are given. **Visual Vocabulary, Frayer Model, Reverse Frayer, Concept Cards, and Vocabulary Ribbon** are examples that employ forming concepts, comparing and contrasting concepts, and using graphic organizers. **Visual Vocabulary Reflection** provides students with the opportunity to use a R.A.F.T. as they think about the work they did with vocabulary.

Matching Mania

www.gridgamesgalore.com

Overview

Matching Mania (adapted from Texas and Jones, 2013) is a strategy that can be applied in multiple ways. As a pre-assessment tool, this strategy allows teachers to gauge where students are in their understanding of a particular topic or skill, their use of the associated vocabulary, and their development in the Standards of Practice. Embedded in formative instruction, this strategy becomes a quick and easy transitional activity to check students' understanding of specific content or skills. Matching Mania can also be used as a tool to help students build fluencies. It can even be used as a nonthreatening way to engage students in intervention for skills in which they have gaps.

Students match the problems with the various answers and record on a sheet provided. Each activity is run off on card stock and cut into pieces. Nothing else is needed. If the objective is to build fluency or check for fluency, give students both sets of cards. Have the students "create a viable argument" for at least five of the matches. Other students' arguments could also be shared and critiqued. To focus on problem solving, give the students only the problem cards. Have them determine the solutions, explain their strategy, and justify their reasoning. They then check their work using the answer cards provided. In cases where there are multiple matches to be made, it is best to initially give the students only one set of cards to match at a time. Later, multiple sets can be used as students' proficiency develops.

Matching Mania was developed by Melisa Rice and is being shared with permission. Additional card sets and topics for mathematics can be found at www.gridgamesgalore.com.

Directions

1. All student recording sheets are numbered down the left side with the problem number correlating to the problem number found in the upper left corner of the problem cards.
2. Copy each set of cards within the activity on different colored paper or card stock. This will allow students to easily differentiate the problem cards from the answer cards.
3. Matching Mania requires time in cutting out each activity. You might seek parent volunteers or perhaps student groups that can do this as part of community service hours, or you can have your students cut out the problems and solutions as they work.
4. There are several ways to organize the materials for efficient storage. Use zipper lock quart-size bags to store each set of Matching Mania activity cards. Use gallon bags to store all the individual activity cards, as well as extra recording sheets and the answer key.

Guided Facilitation

Teachers can use Matching Mania as a pre-assessment strategy to gauge students' understanding of concepts. Embedded in formative instruction, this strategy becomes a quick and easy transitional activity to check students' understanding. Matching Mania can be used as a tool to help students build fluency and to support the development of related standards. It can also be used as a nonthreatening way to engage students in intervention for skills in which they have gaps.

Table 4.2a Matching Mania: Energy Terms. A reproducible version of this tool is available in Appendix C (p. 123).

1. **Wind**	**6.** **Solar**
2. **Propane**	**7.** **Hydropower**
3. **Uranium**	**8.** **Geothermal**
4. **Biomass**	**9.** **Natural Gas**
5. **Coal**	**10.** **Petroleum**

Table 4.2b Matching Mania: Energy Definitions

A. Source or energy in hot springs that are used worldwide for bathing	**F.** Native Americans used this to bake the pottery they made from clay
B. More of this energy is produced in one day than the world uses in one year	**G.** The fastest growing renewable source of energy
C. This accounts for more than half of the electricity generated in the states of Oregon, Washington, and Idaho	**H.** Sources include wood, agricultural products, solid waste, landfill gas and biogas, and biofuels
D. The United States uses more of this than any other energy source	**I.** The fuel most widely used by nuclear plants for nuclear fission
E. Modern hot air balloons use this for fuel	**J.** The early Chinese burned this to get salt from seawater

Table 4.2c Matching Mania: Energy Percentages

a. < 1%	**d.** 5%
a. < 1%	**e.** 8%
b. 1.5%	**f.** 19%
b. 1.5%	**g.** 26%
c. 3%	**h.** 35%

Table 4.2d Matching Mania: Energy Student Recording Sheet

Energy	Definition	Example/Formula
1.		
2.		
3.		
4.		
5.		
6.		
7.		
8.		
9.		
10.		

Checking In Reflection

The following Checking In Reflection can be used for both the Matching Mania and the Grid Games. Students have an opportunity to formatively assess themselves based upon concepts they now understand, questions they still may have, and a plan for moving forward.

Figure 4.1 Checking In Reflection. A reproducible version of this tool is available in Appendix B (p. 114).

Grid Games

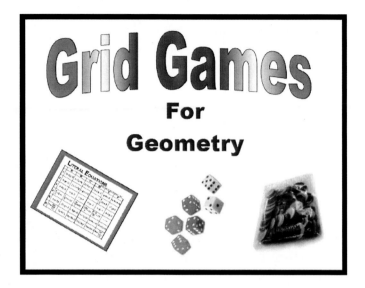

Overview

Grid Games (adapted from Texas and Jones, 2013) is a strategy that creates a nonthreatening environment in which students can practice and build confidence in concept knowledge and understanding through a game. Playing the game itself allows students to develop their critical thinking skills while they are building strategies for capturing a cell or blocking their opponent.

Students answer questions in order to cover a certain number of the cells on the grid sheet. Students can try to cover three in a row, four in a row, or even all the cells on the card to win the game as determined by the teacher.

Grid Games was developed by Melisa Rice and is being shared with permission. Additional card sets and topics for mathematics can be found at www.gridgamesgalore.com.

Directions

Each activity is to be run off on card stock. The other items necessary to play the games are counters or tiles, a number cube, and a letter cube. Use a foam cube or a cube with stick-on labels to make the letter cube. Use the letters A, B, C, D, E, and F.

1. This game is best played in pairs. Each pair of students needs the Grid Game Board for the Grid Game being played, two student recording sheets, a game sheet, a number cube and a letter cube, and

counters of two different colors or double-sided counters. Spinners are also an option instead of the cubes. Provide a number spinner and a letter spinner.

2. Each player rolls the number cube. High roll is Player 1, who begins the game.

3. Player 1 rolls the two cubes and finds the corresponding location on the grid. For example, if Player 1 rolls C5, he locates the fifth square down in the C column.

4. Player 1 then proceeds to answer the question or identify/define what is given in the C5 square and records the answer on the student recording sheet. If he answers the question correctly, he places a colored counter on the C5 square on the game board. If he does not answer correctly, Player 2 may answer the question and cover the square.

5. Player 2 then rolls the two cubes, finds the square indicated, and answers the question. As above, if Player 2 answers the question correctly, she covers it with a colored counter. If she misses it, Player 1 may answer the question.

6. Play continues until a player has a specified number of counters in a row, horizontally, vertically, or diagonally, or has covered the entire grid if that was the goal.

7. If a player rolls the cubes and the square has already been covered, the player will roll again.

Note: If using a game board other than a 6 × 6, when a number is rolled that does not correspond to a grid, the student gets a free choice of grid to solve.

Guided Facilitation

Grid Games serve as nice formative assessments. These games can be modified, through questioning, to support the standards indicated or serve as a pre-assessment option for review. Playing the games helps struggling students as well as students who need some review at any grade level.

1. To conserve resources, two grid games could be run off using the front and back of the card stock. This also allows for differentiation.

2. Putting the grid games in sheet protectors and using two different colors of dry-erase markers eliminates the need for counters.

3. To eliminate the element of chance and to allow students to incorporate strategy, the cubes or spinners are not used. Instead, the students choose where they want to try to claim a cell.

4. If there is a discrepancy in answers, students must "construct a viable argument" or "critique the reasoning of others" to come to consensus.

Table 4.3 Grid Games: World Heritage Sites

	A	B	C	D
Correctly name each World Heritage Site and identify the location of the site.				
1				
2				
3				
4				

A reproducible version of this tool is available in Appendix C (p. 128).
Cell C2: By Herbert Ortner, Vienna, Austria—Own work, CC BY 2.5, https://commons.wikimedia.org/w/index.php?curid=1803669
Cell A4: Source: https://www.flickr.com/photos/allie_k/14721923633/

ABC Sum Race

Overview

The ABC Sum Race (adapted from Texas and Jones, 2013) provides an opportunity for students to "construct viable arguments and critique the reasoning of others." This activity involves students working in groups to answer questions through a competition. Students work both collaboratively and individually while answering questions. Assigning students a specific letter and providing leveled questions makes the activity easily differentiable. The idea was adapted from a lesson shared by Susie Stark, a teacher at Rock Island High School in Illinois.

Directions

1. Students are placed in groups of three and asked to assign each person a letter (A, B, and C) and to identify a team leader.
2. The team leader comes to the front of the room and gets a task card. The task card contains three questions—questions A, B, and C.
3. Each team member answers the questions that correspond to the letter he or she represents and records the answer on the scorecard.
4. Once all answers are recorded, the team adds the answers or the values assigned to the multiple-choice letter together to get a sum and records it on the scorecard as well. If the answers cannot be combined, then the Sum column is left blank.
5. The team leader brings the scorecard to the teacher to be checked.

If correct, the group moves on to the next task card. If incorrect, the team must redo and resubmit.

Guided Facilitation

◆ The first time through, students must individually answer the question that corresponds to their letter and record the answer on the scorecard. If the group leader is sent back to the group with incorrect answers, the entire team can work together to find the errors and resubmit.

◆ Usually, the first time the team leader submits incorrect answers, the teacher will say that the scorecard has incorrect answers, but not which parts are incorrect. The second time the scorecard is submitted with errors, the teacher will give more specific feedback, such as "Check part B."

◆ Color-code the task cards to keep track of which card each group is answering. If you have access to a color printer, you can color code the problem numbers on the scorecard.

◆ Set a specific length of time for students to work or call time when a group reaches the final task card. It is best to call time before the last task card is completed. This will eliminate winners and ensure everyone continues to work until the end of the activity.

Note: Using your test generation software or existing assessments easily facilitates the creation of cards for this race.

ABC Sum Race: Hot Air, Cold Body©
A reproducible version of this tool is available in Appendix C (pp. 130–132).

Card 1

Calculate the time of death. Add each of the digits for the numerical answer.

    A   Body was discovered at midnight and its temperature was 80° F. Two hours later, it had dropped to 75° F. If the temperature at the crime scene has remained steady at 60° F, when did the person die?

    B   Body was discovered at midnight; body temperature was 90° F. At 1:30 am, the temperature of the body has dropped to 87° F. Crime scene temperature has remained steady at 82° F. When was the person murdered?

    C   A dead body was found at 10:00 p.m. The temperature of the body is taken and found to be 80° F. The room has a constant temperature of 68° F. After evidence from the crime scene is collected (one hour later), the temperature of the body is taken again and found to be 78.5° F. Assuming the victim's body temperature was normal (98.6° F) at the time of death, what time did the victim die?

Card 2

Record the number that corresponds to the title of the position described.

1 = Forensic pathologist
2 = Forensic anthropologist
3 = Forensic entomologist

A   Determines the cause of a person's death
B   Uses bones to determine various features of a person who is dead
C   Also known as a medical examiner

Card 3

Record the number that corresponds to the appropriate classification.

1 = Fact
2 = Opinion
3 = Conclusion

A   The person suffered a horrible death.
B   The cause of death was blunt force trauma.
C   The body was still warm due to the temperature of the room.

Table 4.4 ABC Sum Race Scorecard

	A	B	C	SUM
1				
2				
3				

Table 4.5 ABC Sum Race Answer Key

	A	B	C	SUM
1	7:26 PM record as 15	9:40 PM record as 13	2:59 PM record as 16	44
2	1	2	1	4
3	2	1	3	6

The ABC Sum Race Reflection asks students to reflect on their experience as well as any possible strategies used during the activity.

Figure 4.2 ABC Sum Race Reflection. A reproducible version of this tool is available in Appendix B (p. 115).

 ABC Sum Race Reflection

Complete the following:

Always Be C_____

Always B_____   C_____

A_____   B_____   C_____

Multiple Representation Activity[1]

It is important to encourage students to represent their ideas in ways that make sense to them, even if their first representations are not conventional ones. It is also important that they learn conventional forms of representation to facilitate both their learning of mathematics and their communications with others about mathematical ideas.

(National Council of Teachers of Mathematics, 2000)

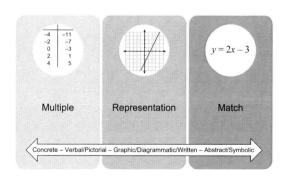

NCTM describes "representation" as referring to both a process and a product. So mathematical representations include all the different ways that students depict their thinking as well as the processes they use to put their thinking into those forms. Mathematical representations can include written work, oral explanations, models with manipulative materials, and even the mental processes one uses to do mathematics. The ways in which mathematical ideas are represented is fundamental to how people understand and use those ideas. Representations have often been taught as an end in and of themselves, mostly as essential elements in supporting students' understanding. When students gain access to mathematical representations and the ideas they express and when they can create representations to capture mathematical concepts or relationships, they acquire a set of tools that significantly expands their capacity to model and interpret physical, social, and mathematical phenomena.

Facilitation Notes

- ◆ Copy the following pages on paper/card stock. Cut apart. (Note: When cutting, you may want to cut off a little extra so students will not be tempted to match cut sides unless you need the visual clue as a modification for some students.)
- ◆ Place one complete set of cards in an envelope/baggie.
- ◆ Prepare one envelope per group. Group size works best at three or four students.
- ◆ Provide each group with a representation strip from the back page as a visual clue.
- ◆ Students then work together to match the representations.
- ◆ Students can then be given the contextual problems and match those to the correct set of representations.
- ◆ Students will then work the contextual problems.

Variations

- ◆ Leave two or three pieces out of the envelope (an equation from one row, a drawing/graph from another, etc.) and have the students generate the missing pieces.
- ◆ If students are working on graphing, leave out all of the graphing pieces and require students to generate the graphs. They could do this with Wikki Stix® for a change of medium.
- ◆ If students are working on writing equations, leave out all of the pieces with the equations and require the students to generate those.

◆ Rewrite more of the equations to NOT be in slope-intercept form if the students need practice on that.

◆ You can color code some of the sets to help students with limited knowledge as they begin the activity.

The MRM Pentagon Reflection (Figure 4.3) offers students the opportunity to reflect on the various forms of representations with which they have just worked and to make connections.

Figure 4.3 Multiple Representation Match Pentagon Reflection. A reproducible version of this tool is available in Appendix B (p. 116).

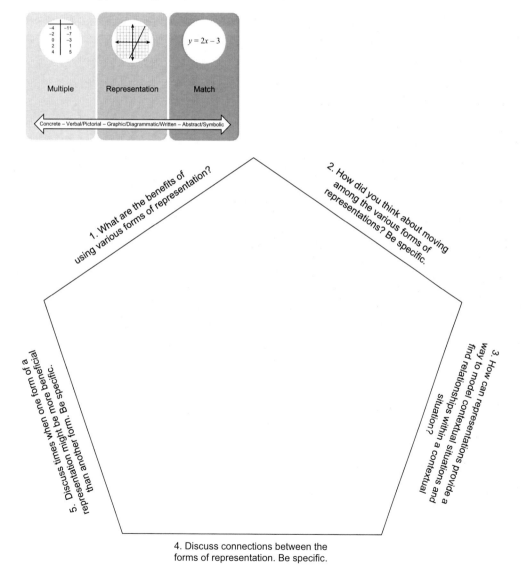

Table 4.6 Multiple Representation Match: Linear Functions. A reproducible version of this tool is available in Appendix C (p. 133).

VERBAL DESCRIPTION	TABULAR REPRESENTATION	GRAPH	SYMBOLIC REPRESENTATION	SET NOTATION	CONTEXTUAL PROBLEM
y is 3 less than twice a number x	x y −4 −11 −2 −7 0 −3 2 1 4 5		$y = 2x - 3y$	{(−4,11),(−2,7), (0,3),(2,1),(4,5)}	Lakisha, a freshman basketball player, scored three less than twice the total number of points of her fellow teammates combined. Write an equation to model this. If Lakisha scored 25 points, how many total points did her teammates score?
y maintains a constant value	x y −4 4 −2 4 0 4 2 4 4 4		$y = 4$	{(−4,4),(−2,4), (0,4),(2,4),(4,4)}	The volume of a tank is four gallons. The tank is now full; however, water is still being poured into the tank for the next three hours. Model, with an equation, the volume of the tank now. Model, with an equation, the volume of the tank in three hours.
the difference of x and y is 4	x y −4 −8 −2 −6 0 −4 2 −2 4 0		$x - y = 4x$	{(−4,−8),(−2,−6), (0,−4),(2,−2),(4,0)}	There are maple trees and poplar trees lining the school driveway. The difference between the number of maples and the poplars is four. What is the least number of each type of tree possible?
half the value of x, when increased by 1, results in the value of y	x y −4 −1 −2 0 0 1 2 2 4 3		$y = \dfrac{1}{2}x + 1$	{(−4,−1),(−2,0), (0,1),(2,2),(4,3)}	Student and adult tickets were sold for the school musical. Twice the number of adult tickets sold was two more than the number of student tickets sold. Model this relationship with an equation in slope-intercept form. How many student tickets were sold if there were at MOST 50 adult tickets sold?
the input for this function is identical to the output	x y −4 −4 −2 −2 0 0 2 2 4 4		$y = x$	{(−4,−4),(−2,−2), (0,0),(2,2),(4,4)}	There are ALWAYS equal amounts of red marbles and blue marbles in the bag. Model this relationship with an equation. If I put three more red marbles in the bag, how many blue marbles do I have to put in the bag?
this function is a direct variation with a constant of variation equal to 3/4	x y −4 −3 −2 −1.5 0 0 2 1.5 4 3		$y = \dfrac{3}{4}x$	{(−4,−3),(−2,−1.5), (0,0),(2,1.5),(4,3)}	A relish recipe requires 3/4 ounce of salt for each pound of cucumbers. Model this relationship with an equation. How many pounds of cucumbers could you pickle with 1 cup of salt?

Table 4.7 Multiple Representation Match Linear Functions Representation Types

VERBAL DESCRIPTION	TABULAR REPRESENTATION	GRAPH	SYMBOLIC REPRESENTATION	SET NOTATION	CONTEXTUAL PROBLEM

Visual Vocabulary

Overview

Building vocabulary is essential, not just for English Language Learners but for all students. Vocabulary is the foundation upon which mathematical understandings develop. Precise use of vocabulary, symbols, and notations is foundational to successfully implementing all of the Standards of Practice. The Visual Vocabulary strategy (adapted from Texas and Jones, 2013) involves students representing their understanding of vocabulary words, phrases, and symbols. The idea was adapted from a lesson shared by Julia Hayes, Newport News, Virginia.

Directions

- ◆ Teams will be given a card identifying a content-related word or phrase. If the classroom has a topical word wall, these words or phrases will come from there.
- ◆ Teams will illustrate the concept or meaning of the word or phrase without using numbers, variables, or other words. This is not Pictionary®: the illustrations should convey meaning, not clues for "guessing the word."
- ◆ A gallery walk will be conducted to identify the words. The drawings can be numbered and the students can record the number and the word or phrase they believe is being represented.
- ◆ Drawings will be posted. Placing these with the words from the word wall will allow students to continue working with these throughout the next unit as well. Students can also replicate these in the student glossary they are developing.

Guided Facilitation

Assessment Activity

1. Upon completing the vocabulary illustration activity, create a set of cards displaying the vocabulary word or phrase, a visual representation of the word or phrase, and its definition.

2. Give each student (or group of students) a set of cards.
3. Students must match their cards appropriately.

Extension Activity

1. Once the students have matched their cards correctly, they will record the vocabulary word or phrase, the visual representation of the word or phrase, and its definition using a vocabulary concept map, such as a Frayer Model (Figure 4.4).
2. Students will then define characteristics of the word or phrase and create a visual counterexample. (At this point, students are allowed to use multiple representations.)

> One of the benefits of the Frayer Model is that it includes counterexamples. It is just as important in developing understanding of new terms that students understand what something is *not* as well as what it is.

One way to engage students in both a reflection as well as an opportunity for writing is to use the following Visual Vocabulary Reflection (see Figure 4.5), which utilizes a R.A.F.T.

Figure 4.4 Renewable Energy Frayer Model. A reproducible version of this tool is available in Appendix B (p. 113).

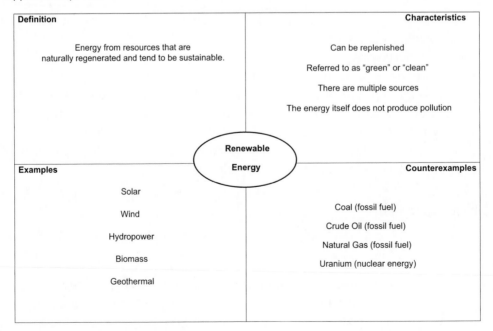

Definition	Characteristics
Energy from resources that are naturally regenerated and tend to be sustainable.	Can be replenished Referred to as "green" or "clean" There are multiple sources The energy itself does not produce pollution

Renewable Energy

Examples	Counterexamples
Solar Wind Hydropower Biomass Geothermal	Coal (fossil fuel) Crude Oil (fossil fuel) Natural Gas (fossil fuel) Uranium (nuclear energy)

Figure 4.5 R.A.F.T. Visual Vocabulary Reflection. A reproducible version of this tool is available in Appendix B (p. 117).

INTEROFFICE MEMORANDUM

To: My Teacher

From: Your Student

Subject: Visual Vocabulary

Date:

CC: My ELA teacher

Vocabulary Ribbon Facilitation

Students use the ribbon to review terms from content or as a pre-assessment check for vocabulary. Students can do the activity in pairs or as teams.

The first student or member of the team writes the first word in the ribbon except for the last letter. They write the last letter of each word in the tail of the ribbon (see Figure 4.6). That letter begins the next word. Students discuss the first word with their partners or teams. Once the team has agreed on what the word means, the next player takes a turn.

Figure 4.6 Vocabulary Ribbon. A reproducible version of this tool is available in Appendix B (p. 119).

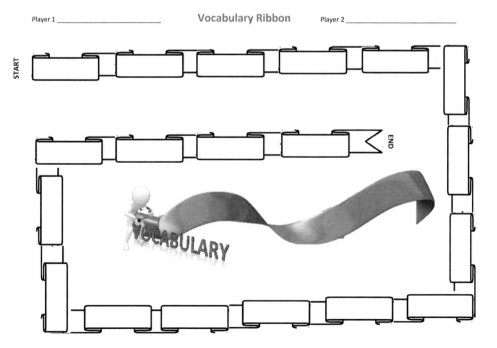

This is adaptable to any discipline because students are generating the words. It can be done in a single class where students pull content-specific vocabulary, but the true power lies in its use to connect vocabulary that transcends disciplines.

The Reverse Frayer & Concept Card

Two other adaptations of the Frayer that provide students opportunities to practice to build proficiency with vocabulary are the Reverse Frayer (Figure 4.7) and the Concept Card (Figure 4.8). The Reverse Frayer is just what it sounds like. The Frayer Model is complete except for the central word. Students use the information given to determine the word or term described.

The Concept Card is similar, with the word on the back of the card and the front divided into four sections. The sections can organize whatever is desired. This is an example from a STEM Activity in which students are determining the time of death based upon the decomposition of the body. The term "decomposition" is on the back of the card.

Figure 4.7 Apples in a Bowl Reverse Frayer

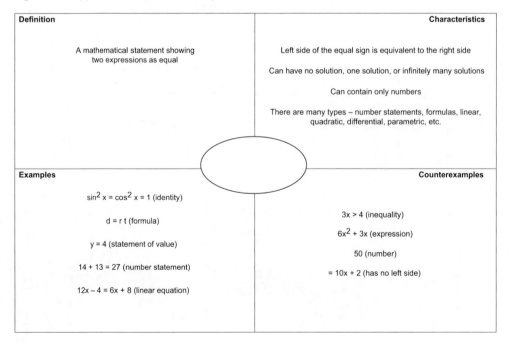

Figure 4.8 Decomposition Concept Card

Definition	Stages
The process of decaying or rotting	**Stages** General Stages ◆ fresh ◆ bloat ◆ active decay ◆ advanced decay ◆ dry/remains Chemical Stages ◆ autolysis ◆ putrefaction
Factors ◆ Temperature ◆ Humidity ◆ Season ◆ Cause of death ◆ Location of the body—surface, soil type ◆ Access by scavengers ◆ Body size and weight ◆ Clothing	**Related Fields** Forensic Pathology Forensic Anthropology Forensic Entomology

Note

1. All Multiple Representation Activities are used with permission of Tammy L. Jones, TLJ Consulting Group.

Bibliography

National Council of Teachers of Mathematics. (2000). *Principles and Standards for School Mathematics*. Reston, VA: National Council of Teachers of Mathematics.

Texas, L. A. and Jones, T. L. (2013). *Strategies for Common Core Mathematics: Implementing the Standards for Mathematical Practice, 9–12*. New York: Routledge.

5

Navigating the Journey:
Staying the Course

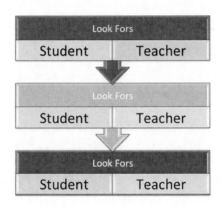

"How do students know that they know?" is a question with which both students and teachers have struggled. Knowing what to look for as students engage in logical reasoning as well as how teachers are providing facilitation aids stakeholders in monitoring accountability for instruction.

The Three Phases of Logical Reasoning Questions & Look Fors

In Chapter 2, we discussed a structure for developing deeper understanding through logical reasoning and introduced several tools for growing students' capacity to engage in problem solving/logical reasoning. These tools include

Figure 5.1 Strategic Journey for Building Logical Reasoning

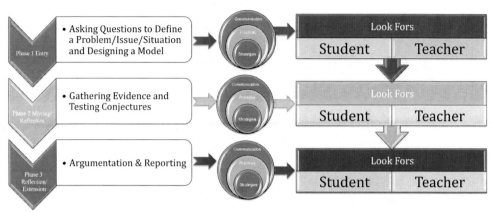

the Logical Reasoning Process Graphic Organizer, Opportunities for Questioning, and the Q-Pyramid and Overlay.

The Three Phases of Logical Reasoning Questions & Look Fors (see Figure 5.1) is a structure that guides both the teacher and the student in what successful implementation of these tools involves. It also serves as a guide for administrators in gathering evidence during teacher observations. In addition, this structure serves as reflection for both students and teachers. These questions and look fors by phase are listed below.

Questions & Look Fors

LRP Phase 1

Questions

◆ What is the problem asking?
◆ How might you identify from the text the problem, question, or dilemma?
◆ How can the scenario be restated as an answer statement?

Look Fors

Students:

◆ are reading and comprehending texts across a range of types and disciplines.
◆ are actively engaged in authentic problem solving vs. simply solving problems.

◆ are actively engaged in scientific inquiry by defining the problem to be solved.

Teachers:

◆ choose and plan for opportunities for students to be engaged in authentic, rigorous, and rich experiences that meet the needs of a diverse population.
◆ prepare by first engaging in the student experience themselves to determine where students might encounter difficulties and by developing questions that will help move both the learner and the learning forward.
◆ provide time for and facilitate discourse around the reading and understanding needed to identify the problem, question, or dilemma.

LRP Phase 2

Questions

◆ What information do you know?
◆ What additional information might be needed?
◆ What vocabulary or symbols need to be defined?
◆ What pattern(s) and/or relationship(s) do you see?
◆ What strategy(ies) could be used here? Why?
◆ How might you model the situation?
◆ How might you identify the different types of evidence needed to support your argument, proposal, or solution?

Look Fors

Students:

◆ can discern pertinent information from that which is not.
◆ ". . . read purposefully . . . to gain both general knowledge and discipline-specific expertise." (CCSS-ELA Student Portrait 2)
◆ are reading and interpreting technical text to recognize the salient ideas.
◆ can understand the context of the problem and the quantities involved as well as how to work with the quantities.
◆ identify the specific types of evidence required by different disciplines.
◆ ". . . state the goal(s) of an investigation, predict outcomes, and plan a course of action that will provide the best evidence to support their conclusions." (NGSS Practice 8)
◆ ". . . decide which variables should be treated as results or outputs, which should be treated as inputs and intentionally varied from trial to trial . . ." (NGSS Practice 8)

◆ use pattern(s)/relationship(s) to create a model (using various representations).
◆ extend known patterns and/or relationships and structures to refine the strategy/plan.

Teachers:

◆ provide a wide range of subject matter from multiple sources that are of "quality and substance" for students to read.
◆ provide a range of ideas and problem situations that encourage varied solution paths.
◆ provide opportunities that create a need for students to develop a plan, strategy, or analysis.
◆ provide time for students to engage in planning and creation of a plan, strategy, or analysis.
◆ support students with specific feedback that will move the learner and learning forward. (Wiliam and Thompson, 2007)

LRP Phase 3

Questions

◆ How did I think about this?
◆ Is my answer reasonable and/or mathematically sound? How do I know?
◆ Does this argument make sense?
◆ How do I know I have sufficiently supported my conclusion(s) with evidence and cited sources as needed?
◆ How might my peers critique my reasoning?
◆ How could I demonstrate a counterexample/counterargument?
◆ Why is my answer reasonable?
◆ How does my answer satisfy the question posed?
◆ Where might I find more resources if needed?
◆ Is my model sufficient for this situation? Why or why not?

Look Fors

Students:

◆ ". . . are expected to become more systematic and careful in their methods." (NGSS Practice 3)
◆ are choosing and using appropriate tools strategically.
◆ are designing solutions/conclusions to problems, questions, and/or dilemmas.
◆ ". . . convey intricate or multifaceted information." (CCSS-ELA Student Portrait 1)

- "... refine and share their knowledge through writing and speaking." (CCSS-ELA Student Portrait 2)
- "adapt their communication in relation to audience, task, purpose, and discipline." (CCSS-ELA Student Portrait 3)
- refine their model as needed.

Teachers:

- allow students opportunities to engage in the process of argumentation.
- provide access to necessary resources.
- monitor student work to provide feedback to make sure students are on track toward the outcome.
- plan deliberately and intentionally to include critical skills needed in creating a valid report.
- create situations that call for students to communicate information, evidence, and ideas in multiple ways. (NGSS Practice 8)

A reproducible version of this tool is available in Appendix A (pp. 96–98).

Strategies for Using the Three Phases of Logical Reasoning Look Fors

Students

In order to explicitly share expectations with students and to help them understand the criteria needed to demonstrate proficiency with respect to logical reasoning, the student look fors can be given as a guide. This document can be placed in their Journey's Notebook and referenced frequently. It can also serve as an outline for collecting evidence of work that demonstrates these skills. At the end of the term or year, these artifacts can be organized into a showcase portfolio that serves as part of a senior project, arranged into a student portfolio to be taken to the next grade, shared as a resource for student-led conferences, or used for a variety of other authentic purposes. Students could also reflect frequently on where they are in the development of these skills and use those reflections to develop an action plan for continued growth.

Teachers

The teacher look fors criteria can be used to guide the lesson planning process and ensure teachers are building opportunities for students to engage in the logical reasoning process on a regular basis and in a variety of contexts. Teachers can use the student look fors to gather evidence to provide students with feedback on their development of logical reasoning and offer suggestions for moving their progress forward.

Teacher Leaders and Instructional Coaches

The powerful part of this process is that it contains a unifying set of tools that can be used across the curriculum and across the grade levels. Having a **common language** among the students, staff, and administration that supports a school-wide or district-wide focus on developing students' logical reasoning skills and building **independent thinkers** opens the door to many opportunities for professional development and coaching. The questions outlined in the LRP phases above could actually be introduced in a staff development session by posing an authentic question/dilemma/scenario facing the staff that needs to be resolved. By engaging in an adult logical reasoning process centered around the phases of the LRP and the driving questions in each, actively participating in the process will allow teachers to experience it firsthand. From there, generalizing the process by sharing the LRP Graphic Organizer, Opportunities for Questioning, Q-Pyramid, and Overlay as tools to develop this process in students will make sense. Using the tasks in Chapter 3 as models will give teachers a starting point as they begin to develop their own (see Table 5.1).

The teacher look fors can be used in coaching teachers throughout the planning process as well as during classroom visits when providing support during implementation. This language helps provide a framework for planning and focus for instruction. Utilizing the look fors can also help facilitate the establishment of a teacher growth plan. This can be for master teachers who are looking to expand their toolkit as well as beginning teachers who need a structure for getting started.

Administrators

The look fors can also be used with administrators to help guide the conversation about what they should be looking for as they are walking through classrooms on a daily basis as well as during evaluative visits. These tools can be used to gather evidence that will help support conversations with teachers and provide guidance for moving their practice further. This process also provides a modeling opportunity of what is expected when they are working to support students through the process as well.

All of these elements are organized into a table. The table correlates the Phases of the Logical Reasoning Process, Opportunities for Questioning, Strategies to Support Logical Reasoning, Content Practices (mathematics, English language arts, science, and social studies), and the Student/Teacher Look Fors.

Table 5.1 The Three Phases of the Logical Reasoning Process

PHASES	QUESTIONING OPPORTUNITIES	STRATEGIES	PRACTICES*	LOOK FORS	
				Students:	Teachers:
Phase 1	Entry (LRP #1) 1. What is the problem asking? 2. How might you identify from the text the problem, question, or dilemma? 3. How can the scenario be restated as an answer statement?	Vocabulary Strategies	M: 1, 2, 4, 5, 6 E: 1, 4, 7 S: 1, 2 SS: 1, 4	◆ are reading and comprehending texts across a range of types and disciplines. ◆ are actively engaged in authentic problem solving (instead of simply solving problems). ◆ are actively engaged in scientific inquiry by defining the problem to be solved.	◆ choose and plan for opportunities for students to be engaged in authentic, rigorous, and rich experiences that meet the needs of a diverse population. ◆ prepare by first engaging in the experience themselves to determine where students might encounter difficulties and to develop questions that will help move both the learner and the learning forward. ◆ provide time for and facilitate discourse around the reading and understanding needed to identify the problem, question, or dilemma.

PHASES	QUESTIONING OPPORTUNITIES	STRATEGIES	PRACTICES*	LOOK FORS	
				Students:	**Teachers:**
Phase 2	Moving/Reflection (LRP #2/#3) 1. What information do you know? 2. What additional information might be needed? 3. What vocabulary or symbols need to be defined? 4. What pattern(s) and/or relationship(s) do you see? 5. What strategy(ies) could be used here? Why? 6. How might you model the situation? 7. How might you identify the different types of evidence needed to support your argument, proposal, or solution?	Building Fluency Strategies Writing Reflections Creating Viable Arguments	M: 1, 2, 4, 5, 6, 7, 8 E: 1, 3, 6 S: 3, 4, 5 SS: 1, 2	• can discern pertinent information from that which is not. • "…read purposefully…to gain both general knowledge and discipline-specific expertise." (CCSS-ELA Student Portrait 2) • are reading and interpreting technical text to recognize the salient ideas. • can understand the context of the problem and the quantities involved as well as how to work with the quantities. • identify the specific types of evidence required by different disciplines. • "…state the goal(s) of an investigation, predict outcomes, and plan a course of action that will provide the best evidence to support their conclusions." (NGSS Practice 8) • "…decide which variables should be treated as results or outputs, which should be treated as inputs and intentionally varied from trial to trial." (NGSS Practice 8) • use pattern(s)/relationship(s) to create a model (using various representations). • extend known patterns and/or relationships and structures to refine the strategy/plan.	• provide a wide range of subject matter from multiple sources that is of "quality and substance" for students to read. • provide a range of ideas and problem situations that encourage varied solution paths. • provide opportunities that create a need for students to develop a plan, strategy, or analysis. • provide time for students to engage in planning and creation of a plan, strategy, or analysis. • support students with specific feedback that will move the learner and learning forward. (Wiliam and Thompson, 2007)

(Continued)

Table 5.1 (Continued)

PHASES	QUESTIONING OPPORTUNITIES	STRATEGIES	PRACTICES*	LOOK FORS	
				Students:	Teachers:
Phase 3	Reflection/Extension (LRP #4/#5) 1. How did I think about this? 2. Is my answer reasonable and/or mathematically sound? How do I know? 3. Does this argument make sense? 4. How do I know I have sufficiently supported my conclusion(s) with evidence, and cited sources as needed? 5. How might my peers critique my reasoning? 6. How could I demonstrate a counterexample/counterargument? 7. Why is my answer reasonable? 8. How does my answer satisfy the question posed? 9. Where might I find more resources if needed? 10. Is my model sufficient for this situation? Why or why not?	MRM ABC Sum Race Visual Vocabulary (R.A.F.T.) (Reverse Frayer) Writing Reflections	M: 1, 3, 5, 6 E: 1, 2, 3, 4, 5, 6, 7 S: 6, 7, 8 SS: 2, 3, 4	◆ "…are expected to become more systematic and careful in their methods." (NGSS Practice 3) ◆ are choosing and using appropriate tools strategically. ◆ are designing solutions/conclusions to problems, questions, and/or dilemmas. ◆ "…convey intricate or multifaceted information." (CCSS-ELA Student Portrait 1) ◆ "…refine and share their knowledge through writing and speaking." (CCSS-ELA Student Portrait 2) ◆ "…adapt their communication in relation to audience, task, purpose, and discipline." (CCSS-ELA Student Portrait 3) ◆ refine their model as needed.	◆ allow students opportunities to engage in the process of argumentation. ◆ provide access to necessary resources. ◆ monitor student work to provide feedback to make sure students are on track toward the outcome. ◆ plan deliberately and intentionally to include critical skills needed in creating a valid report. ◆ create situations that call for students to communicate information, evidence, and ideas in multiple ways. (NGSS Practice 8)

*M: Math; E: ELA; S: Science; SS: Social Studies

A reproducible version of this tool is available in Appendix A (pp. 99–101).

Bibliography

Common Core State Standards Initiative. (2010). *Students Who Are College and Career Ready in Reading, Writing, Speaking, Listening, and Language.* Retrieved from www.corestandards.org/wp-content/uploads/ELA_Standards1.pdf

Next Generation Science Standards: For States, By States. (2013). Appendix F—Science and Engineering Practices in the NGSS. Retrieved from www.nextgenscience.org/sites/ngss/files/Appendix%20F%20%20Science%20and%20Engineering%20Practices%20in%20the%20NGSS%20-%20FINAL%20060513.pdf

Wiliam, D. and Thompson, M. (2007). Integrating Assessment with Instruction: What Will It Take to Make It Work? In C. A. Dwyer (Ed.), *The Future of Assessment: Shaping Teaching and Learning* (pp. 53–82). Mahwah, NJ: Lawrence Erlbaum Associates.

Appendix A: Logical Reasoning Process Tools and Sample Tasks

Logical Reasoning Process

Figure A.1 Logical Reasoning Process Graphic Organizer

Adapted from: *Strategies for Common Core Mathematics: Implementing the Standards for Mathematical Practice* (Texas and Jones, 2013).

Overview

Logical reasoning has traditionally been a challenge for many students, whether in the primary grades or in high school. Knowing "how to teach" logical reasoning can be an equal challenge for the teacher. One of the difficulties when facilitating logical reasoning lies in the variety of situations that students encounter as well as the multiple strategies that can be applied to resolving them. Another obstacle facing teachers and students is the reading that is required for "making sense of problems." For some students, this is the first roadblock in finding that "entry point" to engage in the situation.

Directions

The following is a logical reasoning process that can be used to assist students in making sense of problems as well as decontextualizing and contextualizing given information. The process also requires students to construct viable arguments as they formulate their own ideas about the meaning of the situation and make predictions about the outcome. Once they obtain a solution, students compare it to the prediction to determine the reasonableness of the solution. By following explicit steps to unpack the problem, students are able to begin the process with minimal to no teacher guidance and complete the initial steps. This eliminates the blank piece of paper or the famous "I don't know" answer. Using a consistent process over time will assist students in becoming more successful with logical reasoning. While this process may not always fit every problem, it does help students develop a systematic approach to finding the entry point into various tasks.

Ideas for Implementing the Logical Reasoning Process Graphic Organizer

- ◆ Individual: Each student is assigned a problem/scenario/dilemma and completes the chart individually as classwork or homework.
- ◆ Individual/Pairs: Students are given a completed chart and must create the problem/scenario/dilemma.
- ◆ Individual/Pairs: Work three or four tasks using the LRP Graphic Organizer. Cut the steps of each task into individual strips and place in an envelope. Give students the envelope and ask them to reassemble the strips to form the problems and solution pathways.

◆ Individual/Pairs: Give students a completed chart that contains errors and have them identify the errors and make corrections.

◆ Partner Pairs: Think-Pair-Share. Allow an initial period of time for each student to read and understand the problem/scenario/dilemma. Then allow partners to discuss and solve the problem together. Students should be prepared to explain their solutions to the class.

◆ Partner Pairs: Same as above, except that students must solve the problem from two solution pathways.

◆ Partner Pairs: Each partner completes steps 1–4 of his or her individually assigned problem/scenario/dilemma. Partners will then exchange papers and complete step 5 by verifying the answer/solution.

◆ Small Group: Each student begins with a problem/scenario/dilemma and does step 1. Upon completion of that step, students hand their paper to the next person in a clockwise (or counterclockwise) rotation. Each student then completes the next step in the problem. The process continues for three more steps until all of the steps of the process have been completed.

Opportunities for Questioning

Figure A.2 Opportunities for Questioning Student Version

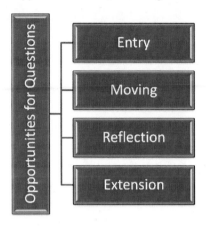

Entry: Getting Started

- ◆ What is the problem asking?
- ◆ How might you identify from the text the problem, question, or dilemma?
- ◆ How can the scenario be restated as an answer statement?

Moving: When Stuck

- ◆ What information do you know?
- ◆ What additional information might be needed?
- ◆ What vocabulary or symbols need to be defined?

Reflection: Thinking about Thinking

- ◆ What pattern(s) and/or relationship(s) exist?
- ◆ What types of evidence are needed to support your reasoning?
- ◆ How does my answer satisfy the question posed?

Extension: Deeper Thinking

- ◆ How would the solution change if the constraints in the situation were changed?
- ◆ Why did . . . ?
- ◆ How might you use the patterns/relationships you identified to make a general conjecture about . . . ?

Puzzling Problems Facilitation Notes

Overview

Puzzling Problems (adapted from Texas and Jones, 2013) involves students in cooperative groups working on a rich task that involves multiple components.

The tasks are scaffolded so each subsequent question in some part depends upon the students completing the prior piece. These were developed to model what a performance-based assessment at a higher cognitive level might resemble. Writing is a key component in each of these scenarios.

This activity is a perfect opportunity for students to employ journaling or a Journey's Notebook to individually record their observations, reasoning, and thoughts as they work through each component of the task. It also gives them a reference for the next component. Teachers need to remember that when students can discuss something verbally, it does not necessarily mean they can capture those thoughts in written words. Writing needs to be a natural, daily part of a student's experiences.

This strategy provides students the opportunity to work through tasks collaboratively. The idea was adapted from a lesson shared by Bob Trammel, a consultant in Indiana.

Directions

1. Enlarge a task to fit on one sheet of card stock. Cut the task into puzzle pieces. The number of pieces can correspond to the number of students per group, or you can give each student multiple pieces of the same puzzle.
2. Give each student a puzzle piece or pieces.
3. Students must match their puzzle pieces to form a task to consider.
4. As a learning group, students select a strategy to address the problem/issue.
5. Students resolve the issue as a team and submit a proposal. The team must be able to construct a viable argument for its solution and document it individually as a journal activity.

Guided Facilitation

Multiple Representations

1. For each unit of study, create a set of puzzles. Each puzzle will contain multiple pieces with each piece displaying a different representation of the same task.

2. Place students in groups of two or three. Each group will receive a set of puzzle pieces.
3. Students must match their pieces appropriately to solve the set of puzzles.

Puzzle Piece Sort (Classification)

1. For each unit of study, create a set of puzzle pieces. Each puzzle piece will display a different example.
2. Place students in groups of two or three. Each group will receive a set of puzzle pieces.
3. Students must sort and classify all their puzzle pieces.

Equivalency Match

1. For each unit of study, create a set of puzzles. Each puzzle will comprise two pieces.
2. Each piece of the puzzle will display a different representation of an equivalent quantity/concept.
3. Each pair of students will receive a set of puzzles.
4. Students complete all the puzzles appropriately to show matching equivalencies.

Process Statements

1. Choose several tasks organized around one common concept. Work through each task.
2. Create a puzzle for each task. Each piece of the puzzle will display a different step in resolving the issue/problem from problem statement to solution.
3. Place students in groups of two or three. Each group will receive a set of puzzles.
4. Students complete all the puzzles appropriately to display the problem, process statements, and solution.

QUAD Reflection for Puzzling Problems

Q: Question
What questions do you still have about the task?

U: Understanding
What do you now understand after working with this task?

A: Activate
How did this task activate you as a learning resource for a peer (or activate a peer as a resource for you)?

D: Discourse
What discourse did working this task prompt?

Q-Pyramid and Overlay

For class sets of pyramids and overlays, please contact info@TexasAnd Jones.com.

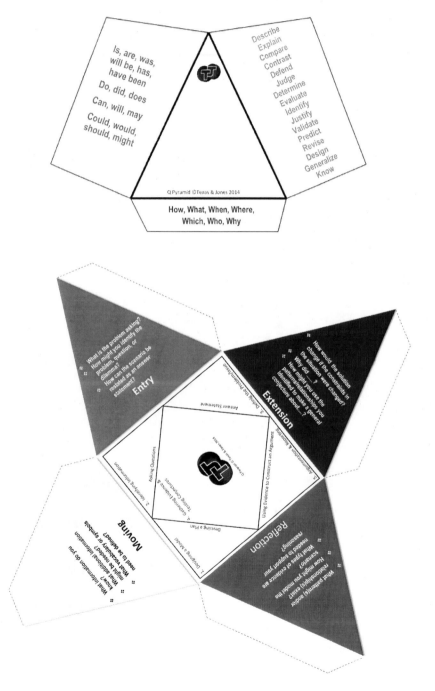

Sample Tasks

Apples in a Bowl Task Card

One night Father Jones couldn't sleep, so he went down into the kitchen, where he found a bowl full of apples. Being hungry, he took 1/6 of the apples.

Later that same night, Mother Jones was hungry and couldn't sleep. She, too, found the apples and took 1/5 of what Father Jones had left.

Still later, Baylan, the oldest Jones son, awoke, went to the kitchen, and ate 1/4 of the remaining apples.

Even later, his brother, Eson, ate 1/3 of what was then left.

Finally, the third son, Kensen, ate 1/2 of what was left, leaving only three apples for Grandmother Jones to use to make a pie.

How many apples were originally in the bowl?

Apples in a Bowl Task-Specific Questions

Entry

1. How many apples were left in the bowl? How does knowing this help you determine how many apples Kensen had in the bowl?
2. What might be a reasonable range of possible answers?

Moving

1. When working with fractions, how do you know if you are multiplying or dividing?
2. What role do grouping symbols play in the equation?
3. What representation do you think would be more efficient in helping you model the situation?

Reflection

1. Does your answer seem reasonable? Why or why not?
2. What do you think are the most common mistakes people make when doing this problem?

Extension

1. How could you represent the problem as a single equation?
2. How would the problem be affected if the fractional pieces did not have consecutive denominators?

Hot Air, Cold Body: Using Newton's Law of Cooling to Determine Time of Death Task Card[1]

Use Newton's law of cooling to narrow down the number of suspects by determining when the victim was killed. This activity is used with permission by Texas Instruments, Inc. The TI-Nspire Activity Files, Student Worksheets, and Teacher Notes can be downloaded from: https://education.ti.com/en/tisciencenspired/us/forensics/case-files.

Memo to Detective Sergeant

The elevator operator of the Ritz Palace Hotel died from a stab wound while on duty last Thursday evening. His body was discovered by a family on its way down to the pool. When we arrived at the scene, we canvassed the area but found nothing. The elevator is full of fingerprints of the hundreds of guests who ride it during the day. We have several suspects in mind, but we are having trouble pinning down the time of death. If we can determine that, we have a good shot at finding the killer.

Enclosed are a photograph of the crime scene and part of the paramedic report.

Paramedic report
Date: 10/5/05
Time: 9:45 p.m.
Body temperature: 29.0°C
Notes: Elevator temperature was high; thermostat set at 27°C.

Hot Air, Cold Body: Using Newton's Law of Cooling to Determine Time of Death©
Task-Specific Questions

Entry

1. What information from the crime scene do you know? How can it be verified?
2. What additional information, if any, might you need to know? Why?

Moving

1. What type of model do you think you will use to determine the coefficient of cooling?
2. If using a graph as your model, how will the calculator's/handheld's window settings be a factor?

Reflection

1. Does/Do your answer(s) seem reasonable? Why or why not?
2. Identify and discuss any possible source(s) of error in your model and/or calculations.
3. What role do units have in the work you did to determine the final answer?

Extension

1. The experiment used to model the crime scene was not a true replica of the actual crime scene. What are some other factors that might have affected the actual cooling rate? Explain in detail.
2. How could the estimate for the time of death be affected if the person had died outside on a cold day? What if they had been sick before they died and had a fever?
3. What are other possible methods of determining the time of death other than through body temperature and the benefits and limitations of each?

Stories from the Past: World Heritage Sites Task Card[2]

According to UNESCO, "The idea of creating an international movement for protecting heritage emerged after World War I. The 1972 Convention concerning the Protection of the World Cultural and Natural Heritage developed from the merging of two separate movements: the first focusing on the preservation of cultural sites, and the other dealing with the conservation of nature."[2]

Research the Strategic Objectives—the "Five Cs" of the World Heritage Convention. Prepare a presentation to report your findings.

Create a "Top 10" list of World Heritage Sites. Validate the reasoning behind your "Top 10" list, being sure to cite primary sources. Include a map showing the locations for your "Top 10" list picks. Create a scale model of your top-pick site using an appropriate scale. Include the "Story from the Past" about your top pick.

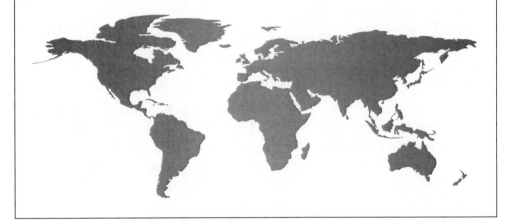

Stories from the Past: World Heritage Sites Task-Specific Questions

Entry

1. What is a World Heritage Site?
2. Why are World Heritage Sites special?
3. What information do you need to know to construct a model? Why?

Moving

1. What type of model do you think you will use to represent your top pick?
2. What factors influence your choice of material for your model?
3. What primary sources are available to find needed information about your site?
4. What calculations will you need to make to build your model?

Reflection

1. How was your choice of your top pick affected by the fact you would have to create a model?
2. What might be possible sources of error in your model and/or calculations? Discuss fully.
3. What role do units have in your work?

Extension

1. How might you compare and contrast the challenges you had in constructing your model vs. the construction of your site—if man-made?
2. How might you compare and contrast the benefits of the medium chosen for the construction of your model with an alternative medium?

Wind Energy: Pros and Cons Task Card

You are the Agricultural Extension Agent for your local district. You have had several calls from local farmers and landowners about the potential development of a wind farm by WindCo in your area. The citizens have asked you to help advise them on this matter. There is a community 4-H meeting next week. You need to do a brief survey of the pros and cons of wind energy and be able to summarize your findings in a presentation at the next community 4-H meeting so the district can make an educated choice.

Wind Energy: Pros and Cons Task-Specific Questions

Entry

1. What is a wind farm?
2. How is wind energy produced?

Moving

1. What is required for a wind farm?
2. Environmentally, is our district a good fit for a wind farm? Why or why not?
3. What are some reputable sources for information about wind farms?

Reflection

1. What criteria is used to determine if a factor is a pro or con?
2. How was credibility for the sources determined? Could there have been any bias? Why or why not?
3. What factors led you to your conclusion?

Extension

1. What would be the feasibility for this project were there no government subsidies?
2. If part of the forest in the local park needs to be used, will the benefit still outweigh the cost?

The Three Phases of Logical Reasoning Questions & Look Fors

Questions & Look Fors

LRP Phase 1

Questions

◆ What is the problem asking?
◆ How might you identify from the text the problem, question, or dilemma?
◆ How can the scenario be restated as an answer statement?

Look Fors

Students:

◆ are reading and comprehending texts across a range of types and disciplines.
◆ are actively engaged in authentic problem solving (instead of simply solving problems).
◆ are actively engaged in scientific inquiry by defining the problem to be solved.

Teachers:

◆ choose and plan for opportunities for students to be engaged in authentic, rigorous, and rich experiences that meet the needs of a diverse population.
◆ prepare by first engaging in the student experience themselves to determine where students might encounter difficulties and by developing questions that will help move both the learner and the learning forward.
◆ provide time for and facilitate discourse around the reading and understanding needed to identify the problem, question, or dilemma.

LRP Phase 2

Questions

◆ What information do you know?
◆ What additional information might be needed?
◆ What vocabulary or symbols need to be defined?
◆ What pattern(s) and/or relationship(s) do you see?

◆ What strategy(ies) could be used here? Why?
◆ How might you model the situation?
◆ How might you identify the different types of evidence needed to support your argument, proposal, or solution?

Look Fors

Students:

◆ can discern pertinent information from that which is not.
◆ ". . . read purposefully . . . to gain both general knowledge and discipline-specific expertise." (CCSS-ELA Student Portrait 2)
◆ are reading and interpreting technical text to recognize the salient ideas.
◆ can understand the context of the problem and the quantities involved as well as how to work with the quantities.
◆ identify the specific types of evidence required by different disciplines.
◆ ". . . state the goal(s) of an investigation, predict outcomes, and plan a course of action that will provide the best evidence to support their conclusions." (NGSS Practice 8)
◆ ". . . decide which variables should be treated as results or outputs, which should be treated as inputs and intentionally varied from trial to trial . . ." (NGSS Practice 8)
◆ use pattern(s)/relationship(s) to create a model (using various representations).
◆ extend known patterns and/or relationships and structures to refine the strategy/plan.

Teachers:

◆ provide a wide range of subject matter from multiple sources that are of "quality and substance" for students to read.
◆ provide a range of ideas and problem situations that encourage varied solution paths.
◆ provide opportunities that create a need for students to develop a plan, strategy, or analysis.
◆ provide time for students to engage in planning and creation of a plan, strategy, or analysis.
◆ support students with specific feedback that will move the learner and learning forward. (Wiliam and Thompson, 2007)

LRP Phase 3

Questions

- How did I think about this?
- Is my answer reasonable and/or mathematically sound? How do I know?
- Does this argument make sense?
- How do I know I have sufficiently supported my conclusion(s) with evidence and cited sources as needed?
- How might my peers critique my reasoning?
- How could I demonstrate a counterexample/counterargument?
- Why is my answer reasonable?
- How does my answer satisfy the question posed?
- Where might I find more resources if needed?
- Is my model sufficient for this situation? Why or why not?

Look Fors

Students:

- ". . . are expected to become more systematic and careful in their methods." (NGSS Practice 3)
- are choosing and using appropriate tools strategically.
- are designing solutions/conclusions to problems, questions, and/or dilemmas.
- ". . . convey intricate or multifaceted information." (CCSS-ELA Student Portrait 1)
- ". . . refine and share their knowledge through writing and speaking." (CCSS-ELA Student Portrait 2)
- ". . . adapt their communication in relation to audience, task, purpose, and discipline." (CCSS-ELA Student Portrait 3)
- refine their model as needed.

Teachers:

- allow students opportunities to engage in the process of argumentation.
- provide access to necessary resources.
- monitor student work to provide feedback to make sure students are on track toward the outcome.
- plan deliberately and intentionally to include critical skills needed in creating a valid report.
- create situations that call for students to communicate information, evidence, and ideas in multiple ways. (NGSS Practice 8)

Table A.1 The Three Phases of the Logical Reasoning Process

PHASES	QUESTIONING OPPORTUNITIES	STRATEGIES	PRACTICES*	LOOK FORS	
				Students:	**Teachers:**
Phase 1	Entry (LRP #1) 1. What is the problem asking? 2. How might you identify from the text the problem, question, or dilemma? 3. How can the scenario be restated as an answer statement?	Vocabulary Strategies	M: 1, 2, 4, 5, 6 E: 1, 4, 7 S: 1, 2 SS: 1, 4	◆ are reading and comprehending texts across a range of types and disciplines. ◆ are actively engaged in authentic problem solving (instead of simply solving problems). ◆ are actively engaged in scientific inquiry by defining the problem to be solved.	◆ choose and plan for opportunities for students to be engaged in authentic, rigorous, and rich experiences that meet the needs of a diverse population. ◆ prepare by first engaging in the experience themselves to determine where students might encounter difficulties and to develop questions that will help move both the learner and the learning forward. ◆ provide time for and facilitate discourse around the reading and understanding needed to identify the problem, question, or dilemma.

(Continued)

Table A.1 (Continued)

PHASES	QUESTIONING OPPORTUNITIES	STRATEGIES	PRACTICES*	LOOK FORS	
				Students:	Teachers:
Phase 2	Moving/Reflection (LRP #2/#3) 1. What information do you know? 2. What additional information might be needed? 3. What vocabulary or symbols need to be defined? 4. What pattern(s) and/ or relationship(s) do you see? 5. What strategy(ies) could be used here? Why? 6. How might you model the situation? 7. How might you identify the different types of evidence needed to support your argument, proposal, or solution?	Building Fluency Strategies Writing Reflections Creating Viable Arguments	M: 1, 2, 4, 5, 6, 7, 8 E: 1, 3, 6 S: 3, 4, 5 SS: 1, 2	◆ can discern pertinent information from that which is not. ◆ "…read purposefully…to gain both general knowledge and discipline-specific expertise." (CCSS-ELA Student Portrait 2) ◆ are reading and interpreting technical text to recognize the salient ideas. ◆ can understand the context of the problem and the quantities involved as well as how to work with the quantities. ◆ identify the specific types of evidence required by different disciplines. ◆ "…state the goal(s) of an investigation, predict outcomes, and plan a course of action that will provide the best evidence to support their conclusions." (NGSS Practice 8) ◆ "…decide which variables should be treated as results or outputs, which should be treated as inputs and intentionally varied from trial to trial." (NGSS Practice 8) ◆ use pattern(s)/relationship(s) to create a model (using various representations). ◆ extend known patterns and/or relationships and structures to refine the strategy/plan.	◆ provide a wide range of subject matter from multiple sources that is of "quality and substance" for students to read. ◆ provide a range of ideas and problem situations that encourage varied solution paths. ◆ provide opportunities that create a need for students to develop a plan, strategy, or analysis. ◆ provide time for students to engage in planning and creation of a plan, strategy, or analysis. ◆ support students with specific feedback that will move the learner and learning forward. (Wiliam and Thompson, 2007)

PHASES	QUESTIONING OPPORTUNITIES	STRATEGIES	PRACTICES*	LOOK FORS	
				Students:	**Teachers:**
Phase 3	Reflection/Extension (LRP #4/#5) 1. How did I think about this? 2. Is my answer reasonable and/ or mathematically sound? How do I know? 3. Does this argument make sense? 4. How do I know I have sufficiently supported my conclusion(s) with evidence, and cited sources as needed? 5. How might my peers critique my reasoning? 6. How could I demonstrate a counterexample/ counterargument? 7. Why is my answer reasonable? 8. How does my answer satisfy the question posed? 9. Where might I find more resources if needed? 10. Is my model sufficient for this situation? Why or why not?	MRM ABC Sum Race Visual Vocabulary (R.A.F.T.) (Reverse Frayer) Writing Reflections	M: 1, 3, 5, 6 E: 1, 2, 3, 4, 5, 6, 7 S: 6, 7, 8 SS: 2, 3, 4	◆ "…are expected to become more systematic and careful in their methods." (NGSS Practice 3) ◆ are choosing and using appropriate tools strategically. ◆ are designing solutions/conclusions to problems, questions, and/or dilemmas. ◆ "…convey intricate or multifaceted information." (CCSS-ELA Student Portrait 1) ◆ "…refine and share their knowledge through writing and speaking." (CCSS-ELA Student Portrait 2) ◆ "…adapt their communication in relation to audience, task, purpose, and discipline." (CCSS-ELA Student Portrait 3) ◆ refine their model as needed.	◆ allow students opportunities to engage in the process of argumentation. ◆ provide access to necessary resources. ◆ monitor student work to provide feedback to make sure students are on track toward the outcome. ◆ plan deliberately and intentionally to include critical skills needed in creating a valid report. ◆ create situations that call for students to communicate information, evidence, and ideas in multiple ways. (NGSS Practice 8)

*M: Math; E: ELA; S: Science; SS: Social Studies

Notes

1. © 2013 Texas Instruments Incorporated.
2. UNESCO, retrieved from http://whc.unesco.org/en/convention/August 31, 2015.

Bibliography

Common Core State Standards Initiative. (2010). *Students Who Are College and Career Ready in Reading, Writing, Speaking, Listening, and Language.* Retrieved from www.corestandards.org/wp-content/uploads/ELA_Standards1.pdf

Next Generation Science Standards: For States, By States. (2013). Appendix F—Science and Engineering Practices in the NGSS. Retrieved from www.nextgenscience.org/sites/ngss/files/Appendix%20F%20%20Science%20and%20Engineering%20Practices%20in%20the%20NGSS%20-%20FINAL%20060513.pdf

Texas, L. A. and Jones, T. L. (2013). *Strategies for Common Core Mathematics: Implementing the Standards for Mathematical Practice 9–12.* New York: Routledge.

Wiliam, D. and Thompson, M. (2007). Integrating Assessment with Instruction: What Will It Take to Make It Work? In C. A. Dwyer (Ed.), *The Future of Assessment: Shaping Teaching and Learning* (pp. 53–82). Mahwah, NJ: Lawrence Erlbaum Associates.

Appendix B: Opportunities for Writing Strategies and Samples

Table B.1 Opportunities for Writing Task Alignment (High School)

Subjects	Task	Visual Vocabulary	Frayer Model/ Graphic Organizer	Compare & Contrast	Writing About	Vocabulary Ribbon	Showing Evidence	Reflecting	Creating Ideas	Inquiry	Making Meaning	Educating	Producing Products	Journey's Notebook
Math	Apples in a Bowl		X		X			QUAD	Logical Reasoning Process: Steps 1–3			X	X	X
Science Math CTE	Hot Air, Cold Body©—TI	Specific to unit of study		X		Can be used at any time	X	QUAD	Logical Reasoning Process: Steps 1–3				X	X
SS ELA Math	Stories from the Past			X	X			QUAD	Logical Reasoning Process: Steps 1–3			X	X	X
CTE SS ELA	Wind Energy		X				X	QUAD	Logical Reasoning Process: Steps 1–3				X	X
		Vocabulary					**Writing Opportunities**							

Table B.2 Opportunities for Writing Task Alignment (Middle School)

Subjects	Task	Visual Vocabulary	Frayer Model/ Graphic Organizer	Compare & Contrast	Writing About	Vocabulary Ribbon	Showing Evidence	Reflecting	Creating Ideas	Inquiry	Making Meaning	Educating	Producing Products	Journey's Notebook
Math	Apples in a Bowl	Specific to unit of study		X		Specific to unit of study	X	QUAD	Logical Reasoning Process: Steps 1–3				X	X
Science Math	Body of Evidence©— TI		X		X			QUAD	Logical Reasoning Process: Steps 1–3			X	X	X
SS Science ELA	Mapping Our World Heritage		X				X	QUAD	Logical Reasoning Process: Steps 1–3				X	X
Science SS ELA	The Power of the Wind			X	X			QUAD	Logical Reasoning Process: Steps 1–3			X	X	X
		Vocabulary					**Writing Opportunities**							

Table B.3 Opportunities for Writing Task Alignment (Elementary School—Intermediate)

Subjects	Task	Visual Vocabulary	Frayer Model/ Graphic Organizer	Compare & Contrast	Writing About	Vocabulary Ribbon	Showing Evidence	Reflecting	Creating Ideas	Inquiry	Making Meaning	Educating	Producing Products	Journey's Notebook
Math	Apples in a Bowl	Specific to unit of study	X		X	Specific to unit of study		QUAD	Logical Reasoning Process: Steps 1–3			X	X	X
Science SS	How Fingerprints Talk			X			X	QUAD	Logical Reasoning Process: Steps 1–3				X	X
SS Science Math	Silenced Songbirds©			X	X			QUAD	Logical Reasoning Process: Steps 1–3			X	X	X
Science Math	Lifting a Lion©		X				X	QUAD	Logical Reasoning Process: Steps 1–3				X	X
		Vocabulary					**Writing Opportunities**							

Table B.4 Opportunities for Writing Task Alignment (Elementary School—Primary)

Subjects	Task	Visual Vocabulary	Frayer Model/ Graphic Organizer	Compare & Contrast	Writing About	Vocabulary Ribbon	Showing Evidence	Reflecting	Creating Ideas	Inquiry	Making Meaning	Educating	Producing Products	Journey's Notebook
Math	Apples in a Bowl		X		X			QUAD	Logical Reasoning Process: Steps 1–3			X	X	X
Science SS Math	Who Am I?			X			X	QUAD	Logical Reasoning Process: Steps 1–3				X	X
SS Math	Map It©	Specific to unit of study		X	X	Specific to unit of study		QUAD	Logical Reasoning Process: Steps 1–3			X	X	X
Science SS Math	Energy		X				X	QUAD	Logical Reasoning Process: Steps 1–3				X	X
		Vocabulary					**Writing Opportunities**							

Frayer Model: Equation

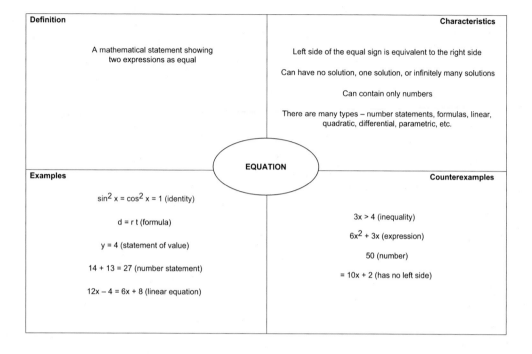

Definition

A mathematical statement showing two expressions as equal

Characteristics

Left side of the equal sign is equivalent to the right side

Can have no solution, one solution, or infinitely many solutions

Can contain only numbers

There are many types – number statements, formulas, linear, quadratic, differential, parametric, etc.

EQUATION

Examples

$\sin^2 x = \cos^2 x = 1$ (identity)

$d = r\,t$ (formula)

$y = 4$ (statement of value)

$14 + 13 = 27$ (number statement)

$12x - 4 = 6x + 8$ (linear equation)

Counterexamples

$3x > 4$ (inequality)

$6x^2 + 3x$ (expression)

50 (number)

$= 10x + 2$ (has no left side)

Figure B.1 Frayer Model

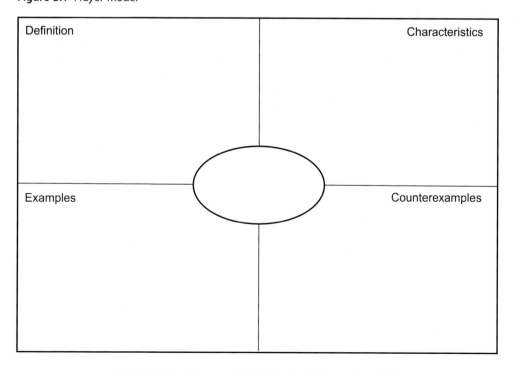

Definition

Characteristics

Examples

Counterexamples

Writing About: Equations

Facilitation

Writing is one of the parts of language that secondary mathematicians are still developing. For some students—those who are ESL/ELL, for example—what they know about mathematics may exceed their ability to communicate it through the written word. For that reason, pictures, diagrams, and the use of manipulatives support the students' efforts in communicating about their mathematical experiences.

Students learn to write by writing, and that writing needs to be original thought, not just copying something that someone else wrote. Therefore, it is imperative that teachers provide opportunities often for students to engage in writing about mathematics, along with an environment that is rich in mathematical language. Providing students with a Journey's Notebook, if for nothing else but the development of a Glossary and a Journal, offers students a place where they can record their thoughts and experiences to chronicle their growth over time while on their educational journey. Students' writing should include discussions about what they did, how they thought—and why they thought or did what they did—and it should use correct academic language. Students' writing should make sense and be complete. This will develop over time for students as they have more opportunities to write about their experiences.

Writing About . . .

Writing About is a small-group writing activity that connects a topic's vocabulary to writing. This is a good activity for struggling students and ESL/ELL who need some support when writing. Give students two or three index cards or scraps of paper. Students study a word cloud for the topic and write one, two, or three sentences about the topic, using words that they find in the word cloud. Students then share their individual sentences in small groups, and each group creates a paragraph about the topic. The index cards allow students to sequence their sentences to build a thoughtful and complete paragraph. They combine similar sentences, check for an introduction and conclusion, add transition words, and so on. This provides an opportunity for students to practice building a paragraph about the topic. This activity can be extended later as an individual writing activity. Note: Invite the ELA teacher to visit the class and share what makes a good paragraph so common expectations can be set that support the work in ELA as well as with the content.

Writing About: Equations and Expressions

Study the word cloud below. Create at least two statements about equations and expressions using the key words you see in the word cloud. With your group, use your sentences to create a paragraph about equations and expressions.

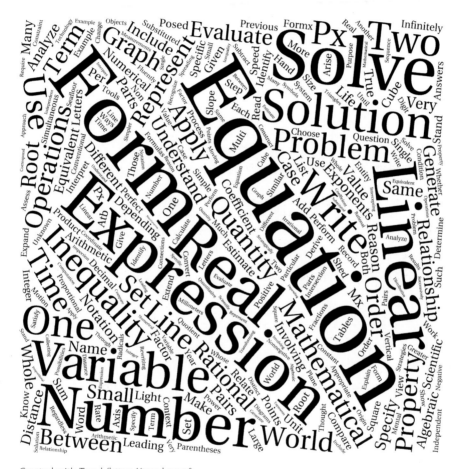

Created with Tagul (https://tagul.com/)

Compare and Contrast: Hot Air, Cold Body

Cooling & Warming	**Forensic & Theoretical**
Logistic graph & Exponential graph	**Evidence & Forensics**
Forensic Scientist & Medical Examiner	**Law of Cooling & Laws of Thermodynamics**
Time of Death & Body Temperature	**Fahrenheit & Celsius**
Celsius & Kelvin	**Model & Analyze**
Constant of cooling & Constant of proportionality	**Forensic entomology & Forensic Pathology**

Compare and Contrast: Stories from the Past

Heritage & Culture	**Rocks & Fossils**
Credibility & Trust	**Conservation & Preservation**
Capacity Building & Strengthening	**Communication & Public Awareness**
Community & Common culture	**Cultural & Natural**
Geographical & Historical	**Cultural Site & Mixed Site**
Monitoring & Neglect	**Primary threat factor & Secondary threat factor**

Writing About: World Heritage Sites

Study the word cloud below. Create at least two statements about World Heritage Sites using the key words you see in the word cloud. With your group, use your sentences to create a paragraph about World Heritage Sites.

Created with Tagul (https://tagul.com/)

Frayer Model: Renewable Energy

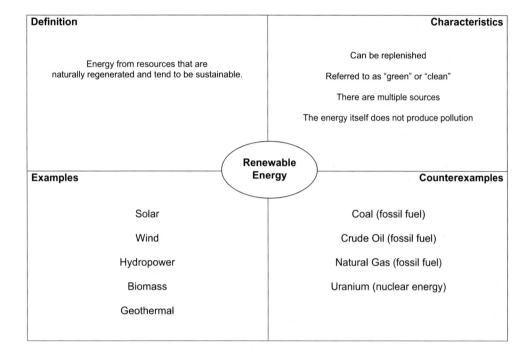

Definition	Characteristics
Energy from resources that are naturally regenerated and tend to be sustainable.	Can be replenished Referred to as "green" or "clean" There are multiple sources The energy itself does not produce pollution

Renewable Energy

Examples	Counterexamples
Solar Wind Hydropower Biomass Geothermal	Coal (fossil fuel) Crude Oil (fossil fuel) Natural Gas (fossil fuel) Uranium (nuclear energy)

Checking In Reflection

What squares with my thinking?

Checking In!

What's still circling around in my head?

What will I change as a result of what I have learned?

ABC Sum Race Reflection

 ABC Sum Race Reflection

Complete the following:

Always Be C_____

Always B_____   C _____

A_____   B_____   C_____

The Multiple Representation Match Pentagon Reflection

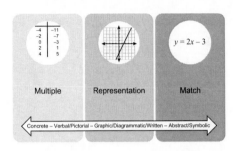

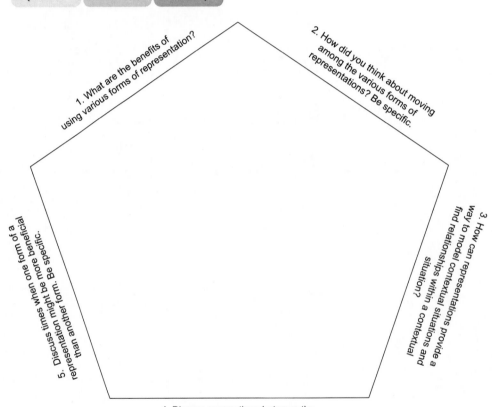

1. What are the benefits of using various forms of representation?

2. How did you think about moving among the various forms of representations? Be specific.

3. How can representations provide a way to model contextual situations and find relationships within a contextual situation?

4. Discuss connections between the forms of representation. Be specific.

5. Discuss times when one form of a representation might be more beneficial than another form. Be specific.

Visual Vocabulary Reflection

INTEROFFICE MEMORANDUM

To:	My Teacher
From:	Your Student
Subject:	Visual Vocabulary
Date:	
CC:	My ELA teacher

Vocabulary Ribbon

Facilitation

Students use the ribbon to review terms from content or as a pre-assessment check for vocabulary. Students can do the activity in pairs or as teams.

The first student or member of the team writes the first word in the ribbon except for the last letter. They write the last letter of each word in the tail of the ribbon (see Figure B.2). That letter begins the next word. Students discuss the first word with their partners or teams. Once the team has agreed on what the word means, the next player takes a turn.

Figure B.2 Vocabulary Ribbon with Sample

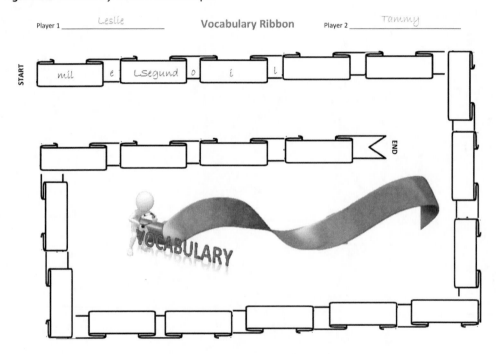

Vocabulary Ribbon

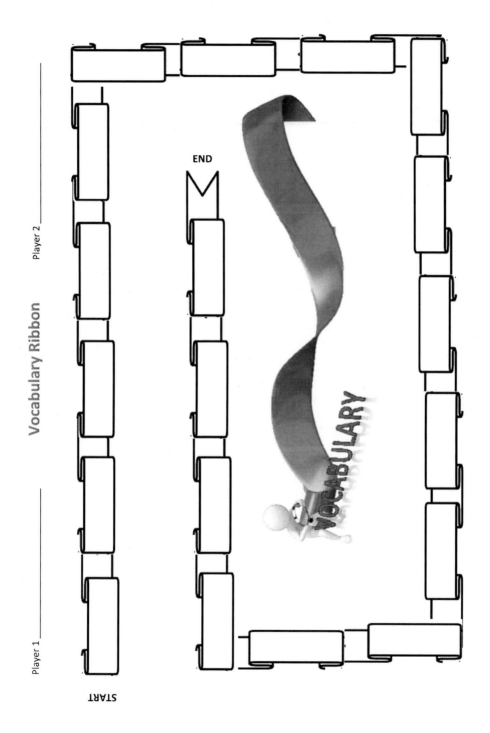

Player 1

Player 2

START

END

Think-Write-Pair-Share

Think-WRITE-Pair-Share

Think about . . .

WRITE about what questions come to mind in the area below.

PAIR with your partner and discuss what each of you wrote.

Be prepared to *SHARE* with the whole group.

Appendix C: Practice to Proficiency Strategies and Samples

Table C.1 Strategies with Task Alignment (High School)

Subjects	Task	Matching Mania	Grid Games	ABC Sum Race	Vocabulary
Math	Apples in a Bowl				
Science Math CTE	Hot Air, Cold Body©—TI			X	Vocabulary strategies are applicable to all subjects: **Visual Vocabulary, Vocabulary Ribbon, Reverse Frayer & Concept Card**
SS ELA Math	Stories from the Past		X		
CTE SS ELA	Wind Energy	X			

Table C.2 Strategies with Task Alignment (Middle School)

Subjects	Task	Matching Mania	Grid Games	ABC Sum Race	Vocabulary
Math	Apples in a Bowl				
Science Math	Body of Evidence©—TI		X		Vocabulary strategies are applicable to all subjects: **Visual Vocabulary, Vocabulary Ribbon, Reverse Frayer & Concept Card**
SS Science ELA	Mapping Our World Heritage			X	
Science SS ELA	The Power of the Wind	X			

Table C.3 Strategies with Task Alignment (Elementary School—Intermediate)

Subjects	Task	Matching Mania	Grid Games	ABC Sum Race	Vocabulary
Math	Apples in a Bowl				Vocabulary strategies are applicable to all subjects: **Visual Vocabulary, Vocabulary Ribbon, Reverse Frayer & Concept Card**
Science SS	How Fingerprints Talk			X	
SS Science Math	Silenced Songbirds©		X		
Science Math	Lifting a Lion©	X			

Table C.4 Strategies with Task Alignment (Elementary School—Primary)

Subjects	Task	Matching Mania	Grid Games	ABC Sum Race	Vocabulary
Math	Apples in a Bowl				Vocabulary strategies are applicable to all subjects: **Visual Vocabulary, Vocabulary Ribbon, Reverse Frayer & Concept Card**
Science SS Math	Who Am I?		X		
SS Math	Map It©			X	
Science SS Math	Energy	X			

Energy Matching Mania

Table C.5 Energy Terms

1. Wind	**6. Solar**
2. Propane	**7. Hydropower**
3. Uranium	**8. Geothermal**
4. Biomass	**9. Natural Gas**
5. Coal	**10. Petroleum**

Table C.6 Energy Definitions

A. Source or energy in hot springs that are used worldwide for bathing	**F.** Native Americans used this to bake the pottery they made from clay
B. More of this energy is produced in one day than the world uses in one year	**G.** The fastest growing renewable source of energy
C. This accounts for more than half of the electricity generated in the states of Oregon, Washington, and Idaho	**H.** Sources include wood, agricultural products, solid waste, landfill gas and biogas, and biofuels
D. The United States uses more of this than any other energy source	**I.** The fuel most widely used by nuclear plants for nuclear fission
E. Modern hot air balloons use this for fuel	**J.** The early Chinese burned this to get salt from seawater

Table C.7 Energy Percentages

a. < 1%	**d. 5%**
a. < 1%	**e. 8%**
b. 1.5%	**f. 19%**
b. 1.5%	**g. 26%**
c. 3%	**h. 35%**

Table C.8 Energy Answer Key

Energy	Fact	Consumption
1. Wind	**G.** The fastest growing renewable source of energy	**b.** 1.5%
2. Propane	**E.** Modern hot air balloons use this for fuel	**b.** 1.5%
3. Uranium	**I.** The fuel most widely used by nuclear plants for nuclear fission	**e.** 8%
4. Biomass	**H.** Sources include wood, agricultural products, solid waste, landfill gas and biogas, and biofuels	**d.** 5%
5. Coal	**F.** Native Americans used this to bake the pottery they made from clay	**f.** 19%
6. Solar	**B.** More of this energy is produced in one day than the world uses in one year	**a.** < 1%
7. Hydropower	**C.** This accounts for more than half of the electricity generated in the states of Oregon, Washington, and Idaho	**c.** 3%
8. Geothermal	**A.** Source or energy in hot springs that are used worldwide for bathing	**a.** < 1%
9. Natural Gas	**J.** The early Chinese burned this to get salt from seawater	**g.** 26%
10. Petroleum	**D.** The United States uses more of this than any other energy source	**h.** 35%

Table C.9 Student Recording Sheet

Energy	Definition	Example/Formula
1.		
2.		
3.		
4.		
5.		
6.		
7.		
8.		
9.		
10.		

World Heritage Sites Grid Game

Table C.10 World Heritage Sites Student Card

Correctly name each World Heritage Site and identify the location of the site.			
A	**B**	**C**	**D**
1			
2			
3			
4			

Cell C2: By Herbert Ortner, Vienna, Austria—Own work, CC BY 2.5, https://commons.wikimedia.org/w/index.php?curid=1803669
Cell A4: Source: https://www.flickr.com/photos/allie_k/14721923633/

Table C.11 World Heritage Sites Student Recording Sheet

	A	B	C	D
1				
2				
3				
4				

Table C.12 World Heritage Sites Answer Key

	A	B	C	D
1	Monticello & the University of Virginia Charlottesville, VA, USA	The Great Wall China	Chartres Cathedral Chartres, France, Europe	The Great Sphinx & Khafra's Pyramid Cairo, Egypt
2	Taj Mahal Agra, India	Acropolis Athens, Greece	Semmering Railway Austria	Los Glaciares National Park Argentina
3	Great Barrier Reef Queensland, Australia	Galápagos Islands Ecuador	Tower of Hercules La Coruña Harbour, Spain	Stonehenge Wiltshire, England
4	Mammoth Cave Kentucky, USA	Great Smoky Mountains Gatlinburg, TN	Grand Canyon Arizona, USA	Machu Picchu Cusco Region, Machupicchu District, Peru

ABC Sum Race: Hot Air, Cold Body©

Sample Cards

Card 1

Calculate the time of death. Add each of the digits for the numerical answer.

A   A body was discovered at midnight and its temperature was 80° F. Two hours later, it had dropped to 75° F. If the temperature at the crime scene has remained steady at 60° F, when did the person die?

B   Body was discovered at midnight; body temperature was 90° F.

At 1:30 am, the temperature of the body has dropped to 87° F.

Crime scene temperature has remained steady at 82° F.

When was the person murdered?

C   A dead body was found at 10:00 p.m. The temperature of the body is taken and found to be 80° F. The room has a constant temperature of 68° F. After evidence from the crime scene is collected (one hour later), the temperature of the body is taken again and found to be 78.5° F. Assuming the victim's body temperature was normal (98.6° F) at the time of death, what time did the victim die?

Card 2

Record the number that corresponds to the title of the position described.

1 = Forensic pathologist
2 = Forensic anthropologist
3 = Forensic entomologist

A   Determines the cause of a persons' death
B   Uses bones to determine various features of a person who is dead
C   Also known as a medical examiner

Card 3

Record the number that corresponds to the appropriate classification.

1 = Fact
2 = Opinion
3 = Conclusion

A   The person suffered a horrible death.
B   The cause of death was blunt force trauma.
C   The body was still warm because of the temperature of the room.

Table C.13 Scorecard

	A	B	C	SUM
1				
2				
3				

Table C.14 Answer Key

	A	B	C	SUM
1	7:26 PM record as 15	9:40 PM record as 13	2:59 PM record as 16	44
2	1	2	1	4
3	2	1	3	6

Table C.15 ABC Sum Race Student Recording Sheet

	A	B	C	SUM
1				
2				
3				
4				
5				
6				
7				
8				
9				
10				
11				
12				
13				
14				
15				
16				
17				
18				
19				
20				

Multiple Representation Match: Linear Functions[1]

M ultiple R epresentation A ctivity
Linear Functions

"It is important to encourage students to represent their ideas in ways that make sense to them, even if their first representations are not conventional ones. It is also important that they learn conventional forms of representation to facilitate both their learning of mathematics and their communications with others about mathematical ideas." (NCTM, 2000. *Principals and Standards of School Mathematics*)

NCTM describes "representation" as referring to both a process and a product. So mathematical representations include all the different ways that students depict their thinking as well as the processes they use to put their thinking into those forms. Mathematical representations can include written work, oral explanations, models with manipulative materials, and even the mental processes one uses to do mathematics. The ways in which mathematical ideas are represented is fundamental to how people understand and use those ideas. Representations have often been taught as an end in and of themselves, most as essential elements in supporting students' understanding. When students gain access to mathematical representations and the ideas they express and when they can create representations to capture mathematical concepts or relationships, they acquire a set of tools that significantly expand their capacity to model and interpret physical, social, and mathematical phenomena.

Facilitation Notes:

- Copy the following pages on paper/card stock. Cut apart. (Note: When cutting you might want to cut off a little extra so students will not be tempted to match cut sides unless you need the visual clue as a modification for some students.)
- Place one complete set of cards in an envelope/baggie.
- Prepare one envelope per group. Group size works best with 3 or 4.
- Provide each group with page 6 or the strip from page 6 as a visual clue
- Students then work together to match the representations. This activity can be used over the course of a topic. Begin with just matching two or three pieces then layer the others as students are ready.
- Students can then be given the contextual problems and match those to the correct set of representations.
- Students will then work the contextual problems.

Variations:

- Leave two or three pieces out of the envelope, (an equation from one row, a drawing/graph from another, etc.) and have the students generate the missing pieces.
- If students are working on graphing, leave out all of the graphing pieces and require students to generate the graphs. They could do this with Wikki Stixs® for a change of medium.
- If students are working on writing equations, leave out all of the pieces with the equations and require the students to generate those.
- Rewrite more of the equations to NOT be in slope-intercept form if the students need practice on that.
- You could color code some of the sets to help students with limited knowledge as they begin the activity.

VERBAL DESCRIPTION	TABULAR REPRESENTATION	GRAPH	SYMBOLIC REPRESENTATION	SET NOTATION	CONTEXTUAL PROBLEM
y is 3 less than twice a number x	x: -4, -2, 0, 2, 4 y: -11, -7, -3, 1, 5		$y = 2x - 3$	{(-4,11),(-2,7), (0,3),(2,1),(4,5)}	Lakisha, a freshman basketball player, scored three less than twice the total number of points of her fellow teammates combined. Write an equation to model this. If Lakisha scored 25 points, how many total points did her teammates score?
y maintains a constant value	x: -4, -2, 0, 2, 4 y: 4, 4, 4, 4, 4		$y = 4$	{(-4,4),(-2,4), (0,4),(2,4),(4,4)}	The volume of a tank is four gallons. The tank is now full, however water is still being poured into the tank for the next three hours. Model, with an equation, the volume of the tank now. Model, with an equation, the volume of the tank in three hours.

There are maple trees and poplar trees lining the school driveway. The difference between the number of maples and the poplars is four.

What is the least number of each type of tree possible?

$\{(-4,-8),(2,-6),(0,-4),(2,-2),(4,0)\}$

$$x - y = 4$$

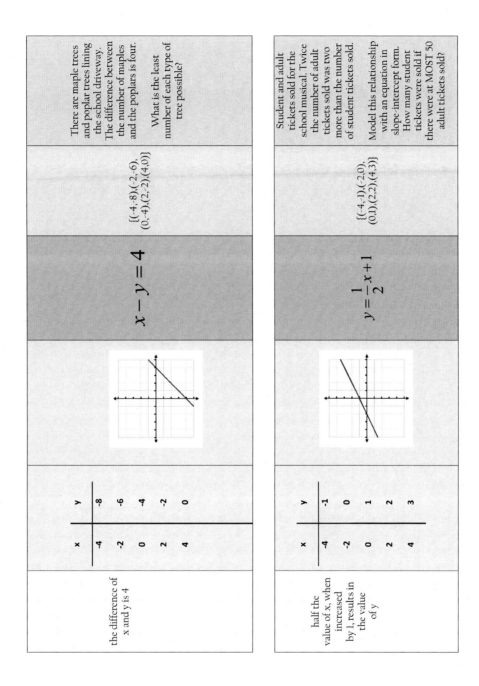

x	y
-4	-8
-2	-6
0	-4
2	-2
4	0

the difference of x and y is 4

Student and adult tickets sold for the school musical. Twice the number of adult tickets sold was two more than the number of student tickets sold.

Model this relationship with an equation in slope-intercept form. How many student tickets were sold if there were at MOST 50 adult tickets sold?

$\{(-4,-1),(-2,0),(0,1),(2,2),(4,3)\}$

$$y = \frac{1}{2}x + 1$$

x	y
-4	-1
-2	0
0	1
2	2
4	3

half the value of x, when increased by 1, results in the value of y

There are ALWAYS equal amounts of red marbles and blue marbles in the bag. Model this relationship with an equation. If I put three more red marbles in the bag, how many blue marbles do I have to put in the bag?

$$\{(-4,-4),(-2,-2),(0,0),(2,2),(4,4)\}$$

$$y = x$$

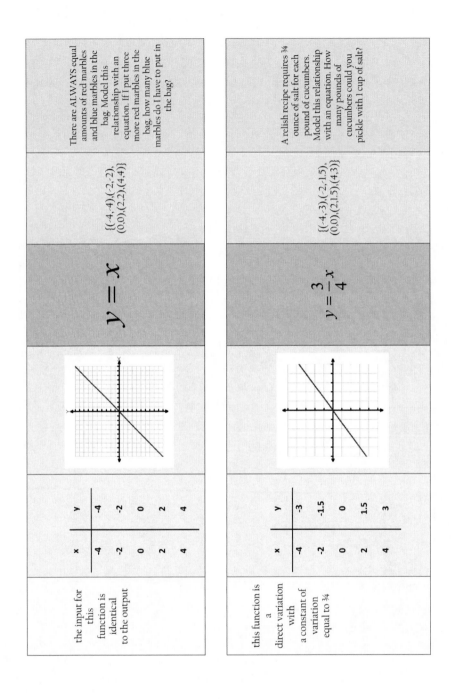

x	y
-4	-4
-2	-2
0	0
2	2
4	4

the input for this function is identical to the output

A relish recipe requires ¾ ounce of salt for each pound of cucumbers. Model this relationship with an equation. How many pounds of cucumbers could you pickle with 1 cup of salt?

$$\{(-4,-3),(-2,-1.5),(0,0),(2,1.5),(4,3)\}$$

$$y = \frac{3}{4}x$$

x	y
-4	-3
-2	-1.5
0	0
2	1.5
4	3

this function is a direct variation with a constant of variation equal to ¾

VERBAL DESCRIPTION	TABULAR REPRESENTATION	GRAPH	SYMBOLIC REPRESENTATION	SET NOTATION	CONTEXTUAL PROBLEM
VERBAL DESCRIPTION	TABULAR REPRESENTATION	GRAPH	SYMBOLIC REPRESENTATION	SET NOTATION	CONTEXTUAL PROBLEM
VERBAL DESCRIPTION	TABULAR REPRESENTATION	GRAPH	SYMBOLIC REPRESENTATION	SET NOTATION	CONTEXTUAL PROBLEM
VERBAL DESCRIPTION	TABULAR REPRESENTATION	GRAPH	SYMBOLIC REPRESENTATION	SET NOTATION	CONTEXTUAL PROBLEM
VERBAL DESCRIPTION	TABULAR REPRESENTATION	GRAPH	SYMBOLIC REPRESENTATION	SET NOTATION	CONTEXTUAL PROBLEM
VERBAL DESCRIPTION	TABULAR REPRESENTATION	GRAPH	SYMBOLIC REPRESENTATION	SET NOTATION	CONTEXTUAL PROBLEM
VERBAL DESCRIPTION	TABULAR REPRESENTATION	GRAPH	SYMBOLIC REPRESENTATION	SET NOTATION	CONTEXTUAL PROBLEM
VERBAL DESCRIPTION	TABULAR REPRESENTATION	GRAPH	SYMBOLIC REPRESENTATION	SET NOTATION	

Note

1. All Multiple Representation Activities used with permission of Tammy L. Jones, TLJ Consulting Group.

Appendix D: Practices from the Academic Standards

Standards for Mathematical Practice

The Standards for Mathematical Practice describe varieties of expertise that mathematics educators at all levels should seek to develop in their students. These practices rest on important "processes and proficiencies" with long-standing importance in mathematics education. The first of these are the NCTM process standards of problem solving, reasoning and proof, communication, representation, and connections. The second are the strands of mathematical proficiency specified in the National Research Council's report *Adding It Up*: adaptive reasoning, strategic competence, conceptual understanding (comprehension of mathematical concepts, operations, and relations), procedural fluency (skill in carrying out procedures flexibly, accurately, efficiently, and appropriately), and productive disposition (habitual inclination to see mathematics as sensible, useful, and worthwhile, coupled with a belief in diligence and one's own efficacy).

1. Make sense of problems and persevere in solving them

Mathematically proficient students start by explaining to themselves the meaning of a problem and looking for entry points to its solution. They analyze givens, constraints, relationships, and goals. They make conjectures about the form and meaning of the solution and plan a solution pathway rather than simply jumping into a solution attempt. They consider analogous problems and try special cases and simpler forms of the original problem in order to gain insight into its solution. They monitor and evaluate their progress and change course if necessary. Older students might, depending on the context of the problem, transform algebraic expressions or change the viewing window on their graphing calculator to get the information they need. Mathematically proficient students can explain correspondences between equations, verbal descriptions, tables, and graphs; draw diagrams of important features and relationships; graph data; and search for regularity or trends. Younger students might rely on using concrete objects or pictures to help conceptualize and solve a problem. Mathematically proficient students check their answers to problems using a different method, and they continually ask themselves, "Does this make sense?" They can understand the approaches of others to solving complex problems and identify correspondences between different approaches.

2. Reason abstractly and quantitatively

Mathematically proficient students make sense of quantities and their relationships in problem situations. They bring two complementary abilities to bear on problems involving quantitative relationships: the ability to *decontextualize*—to abstract a given situation and represent it symbolically and manipulate the representing symbols as if they have a life of their own, without necessarily attending to their referents—and the ability to *contextualize*, to pause as needed during the manipulation process in order to probe into the referents for the symbols involved.

Quantitative reasoning entails habits of creating a coherent representation of the problem at hand; considering the units involved; attending to the meaning of quantities, not just how to compute them; and knowing and flexibly using different properties of operations and objects.

3. Construct viable arguments and critique the reasoning of others

Mathematically proficient students understand and use stated assumptions, definitions, and previously established results in constructing arguments. They make conjectures and build a logical progression of statements to explore the truth of their conjectures. They are able to analyze situations by breaking them into cases and can recognize and use counterexamples. They justify their conclusions, communicate them to others, and respond to the arguments of others. They reason inductively about data, making plausible arguments that take into account the context from which the data arose. Mathematically proficient students are also able to compare the effectiveness of two plausible arguments, distinguish correct logic or reasoning from that which is flawed, and—if there is a flaw in an argument—explain what it is. Elementary students can construct arguments using concrete referents such as objects, drawings, diagrams, and actions. Such arguments can make sense and be correct, even though they are not generalized or made formal until later grades. Later, students learn to determine domains to which an argument applies. Students at all grades can listen or read the arguments of others, decide whether they make sense, and ask useful questions to clarify or improve the arguments.

4. Model with mathematics

Mathematically proficient students can apply the mathematics they know to solve problems arising in everyday life, society, and the workplace. In early grades, this might be as simple as writing an addition equation to describe a situation. In middle grades, a student might apply proportional reasoning to plan a school event or analyze a problem in the community. By high school, a student might use geometry to solve a design problem or use a function to describe how one quantity of interest depends on another. Mathematically proficient students who can apply what they know are comfortable making assumptions and approximations to simplify a complicated situation, realizing that these may need revision later. They are able to identify important quantities in a practical situation and map their relationships using such tools as diagrams, two-way tables, graphs, flowcharts, and formulas. They can analyze those relationships mathematically to draw conclusions. They routinely interpret their mathematical results in the context of the situation and reflect on whether the results make sense, possibly improving the model if it has not served its purpose.

5. Use appropriate tools strategically

Mathematically proficient students consider the available tools when solving a mathematical problem. These tools might include pencil and paper, concrete models, a ruler, a protractor, a calculator, a spreadsheet, a computer algebra system, a statistical package, or dynamic geometry software. Proficient students are sufficiently familiar with tools appropriate for their grade or course to make sound decisions about when each of these tools might be helpful, recognizing both the insight to be gained and their limitations. For example, mathematically proficient high school students analyze graphs of functions and solutions generated using a graphing calculator. They detect possible errors by strategically using estimation and other mathematical knowledge. When making mathematical models, they know that technology can enable them to visualize the results of varying assumptions, explore consequences, and compare predictions with data. Mathematically proficient students at various grade levels are able to identify relevant external mathematical resources, such as digital content located on a website, and use them to pose or solve problems. They are able to use technological tools to explore and deepen their understanding of concepts.

6. Attend to precision

Mathematically proficient students try to communicate precisely to others. They try to use clear definitions in discussion with others and in their own reasoning. They state the meaning of the symbols they choose, including using the equal sign consistently and appropriately. They are careful about specifying units of measure and labeling axes to clarify the correspondence with quantities in a problem. They calculate accurately and efficiently, express numerical answers with a degree of precision appropriate for the problem context. In the elementary grades, students give carefully formulated explanations to each other. By the time they reach high school, they have learned to examine claims and make explicit use of definitions.

7. Look for and make use of structure

Mathematically proficient students look closely to discern a pattern or structure. Young students, for example, might notice that three and seven more is the same amount as seven and three more, or they may sort a collection of shapes according to how many sides the shapes have. Later, students will see 7×8 equals the well-remembered $7 \times 5 + 7 \times 3$, in preparation for learning about the distributive property. In the expression $x^2 + 9x + 14$, older students can see the 14 as 2×7 and the 9 as $2 + 7$. They recognize the significance of an existing line in a geometric figure and can use the strategy of drawing an auxiliary line for solving problems. They also can step back for an overview and shift perspective. They can see complicated things, such as some algebraic expressions, as single objects or as being composed of several objects. For example, they can see $5 - 3(x - y)^2$ as 5 minus a positive number times a square and use that to realize that its value cannot be more than 5 for any real numbers x and y.

8. Look for and express regularity in repeated reasoning

Mathematically proficient students notice if calculations are repeated, and look both for general methods and for shortcuts. Upper elementary students might notice when dividing 25 by 11 that they are repeating the same calculations over and over again, and conclude they have a repeating decimal. By paying attention to the calculation of slope as they repeatedly check whether points are on the line through $(1, 2)$ with slope 3, middle school students might abstract the equation $(y - 2)/(x - 1) = 3$. Noticing the regularity in the way terms cancel when expanding $(x - 1)(x + 1)$, $(x - 1)(x^2 + x + 1)$, and $(x - 1)(x^3 + x^2 + x + 1)$ might lead them to the general formula for the sum of a geometric series. As they work to solve a problem, mathematically proficient students maintain oversight of the process, while attending to the details. They continually evaluate the reasonableness of their intermediate results.

Bibliography

Common Core State Standards Initiative. (2012). *Standards for Mathematical Practice* (pp. 6–8). Retrieved from www.corestandards.org/wp-content/uploads/Math_Standards.pdf

Common Core ELA Student Portraits

The descriptions that follow are not standards themselves but instead offer a portrait of students who meet the standards. . . . As students advance through the grades and master the standards in reading, writing, speaking, listening, and language, they are able to exhibit with increasing fullness and regularity these capacities of the literate individual.

1. They demonstrate independence.

Students can, without significant scaffolding, comprehend and evaluate complex texts across a range of types and disciplines, and they can construct effective arguments and convey intricate or multifaceted information. Likewise, students are able independently to discern a speaker's key points, request clarification, and ask relevant questions. They build on others' ideas, articulate their own ideas, and confirm they have been understood. Without prompting, they demonstrate command of standard English and acquire and use a wide-ranging vocabulary. More broadly, they become self-directed learners, effectively seeking out and using resources to assist them, including teachers, peers, and print and digital reference materials.

2. They build strong content knowledge.

Students establish a base of knowledge across a wide range of subject matter by engaging with works of quality and substance. They become proficient in new areas through research and study. They read purposefully and listen attentively to gain both general knowledge and discipline-specific expertise. They refine and share their knowledge through writing and speaking.

3. They respond to the varying demands of audience, task, purpose, and discipline.

Students adapt their communication in relation to audience, task, purpose, and discipline. They set and adjust purpose for reading, writing, speaking, listening, and language use as warranted by the task. They appreciate nuances, such as how the composition of an audience should affect tone when speaking and how the connotations of words affect meaning. They also know that different disciplines call for different types of evidence (for example documentary evidence in history, experimental evidence in science).

4. They comprehend as well as critique.

Students are engaged and open-minded—but discerning—readers and listeners. They work diligently to understand precisely what an author or speaker is saying, but they also question an author's or speaker's assumptions and premises and assess the veracity of claims and the soundness of reasoning.

5. They value evidence.

Students cite specific evidence when offering an oral or written interpretation of a text. They use relevant evidence when supporting their own points in writing and speaking, making their reasoning clear to the reader or listener, and they constructively evaluate others' use of evidence.

6. They use technology and digital media strategically and capably.

Students employ technology thoughtfully to enhance their reading, writing, speaking, listening, and language use. They tailor their searches online to acquire useful information efficiently, and they integrate what they learn using technology with what they learn offline. They are familiar with the strengths and limitations of various technological tools and mediums and can select and use those best suited to their communication goals.

Science and Engineering Practices in the NGSS

Students appreciate that the 21st-century classroom and workplace are settings in which people from often widely divergent cultures and who represent diverse experiences and perspectives must learn and work together. Students actively seek to understand other perspectives and cultures through reading and listening, and they are able to communicate effectively with people of varied backgrounds. They evaluate other points of view critically and constructively. Through reading great classic and contemporary works of literature representative of a variety of periods, cultures, and worldviews, students can vicariously inhabit worlds and have experiences much different than their own.

Bibliography

Common Core State Standards Initiative. (2010). *Students Who Are College and Career Ready in Reading, Writing, Speaking, Listening, and Language* (pp. 7). Retrieved from www.corestandards.org/wp-content/uploads/ELA_Standards1.pdf

Science and Engineering Practices in the NGSS

The *Framework* uses the term "practices," rather than "science processes" or "inquiry" skills for a specific reason:

> We use the term "practices" instead of a term such as "skills" to emphasize that engaging in scientific investigation requires not only skill but also knowledge that is specific to each practice.
>
> (NRC Framework, 2012, p. 30)

The eight practices of science and engineering that the *Framework* identifies as essential for all students to learn and that it describes in detail are listed below:

1. Asking questions (for science) and defining problems (for engineering)
2. Developing and using models
3. Planning and carrying out investigations
4. Analyzing and interpreting data
5. Using mathematics and computational thinking
6. Constructing explanations (for science) and designing solutions (for engineering)
7. Engaging in argument from evidence
8. Obtaining, evaluating, and communicating information

Practice 1: Asking Questions and Defining Problems

> Students at any grade level should be able to ask questions of each other about the texts they read, the features of the phenomena they observe, and the conclusions they draw from their models or scientific investigations. For engineering, they should ask questions to define the problem to be solved and to elicit ideas that lead to the constraints and specifications for its solution.
>
> (NRC Framework, 2012, p. 56)

Practice 2: Developing and Using Models

> Modeling can begin in the earliest grades, with students' models progressing from concrete "pictures" and/or physical scale models (e.g., a toy car) to more abstract representations of relevant relationships in later grades, such as a diagram representing forces on a particular object in a system.
>
> (NRC Framework, 2012, p. 58)

Practice 3: Planning and Carrying Out Investigations

Students should have opportunities to plan and carry out several different kinds of investigations during their K–12 years. At all levels, they should engage in investigations that range from those structured by the teacher—in order to expose an issue or question that they would be unlikely to explore on their own (e.g., measuring specific properties of materials)—to those that emerge from students' own questions.

(NRC Framework, 2012, p. 61)

Practice 4: Analyzing and Interpreting Data

Once collected, data must be presented in a form that can reveal any patterns and relationships and that allows results to be communicated to others. Because raw data as such have little meaning, a major practice of scientists is to organize and interpret data through tabulating, graphing, or statistical analysis. Such analysis can bring out the meaning of data—and their relevance—so that they may be used as evidence.

Engineers, too, make decisions based on evidence that a given design will work; they rarely rely on trial and error. Engineers often analyze a design by creating a model or prototype and collecting extensive data on how it performs, including under extreme conditions. Analysis of this kind of data not only informs design decisions and enables the prediction or assessment of performance but also helps define or clarify problems, determine economic feasibility, evaluate alternatives, and investigate failures.

(NRC Framework, 2012, p. 61–62)

Practice 5: Using Mathematics and Computational Thinking

Although there are differences in how mathematics and computational thinking are applied in science and in engineering, mathematics often brings these two fields together by enabling engineers to apply the mathematical form of scientific theories and by enabling scientists to use powerful information technologies designed by engineers. Both kinds of professionals can thereby accomplish investigations and analyses and build complex models, which might otherwise be out of the question.

(NRC Framework, 2012, p. 65)

Practice 6: Constructing Explanations and Designing Solutions

The goal of science is to construct explanations for the causes of phenomena. Students are expected to construct their own explanations, as well as apply standard explanations they learn about from their teachers or reading. The Framework states the following about explanation:

> The goal of science is the construction of theories that provide explanatory accounts of the world. A theory becomes accepted when it has multiple lines of empirical evidence and greater explanatory power of phenomena than previous theories.
>
> (NRC Framework, 2012, p. 52)

An explanation includes a claim that relates how a variable or variables relate to another variable or a set of variables. A claim is often made in response to a question and in the process of answering the question, scientists often design investigations to generate data.

The goal of engineering is to solve problems. Designing solutions to problems is a systematic process that involves defining the problem, then generating, testing, and improving solutions. This practice is described in the Framework as follows:

> Asking students to demonstrate their own understanding of the implications of a scientific idea by developing their own explanations of phenomena, whether based on observations they have made or models they have developed, engages them in an essential part of the process by which conceptual change can occur.
>
> In engineering, the goal is a design rather than an explanation. The process of developing a design is iterative and systematic, as is the process of developing an explanation or a theory in science. Engineers' activities, however, have elements that are distinct from those of scientists. These elements include specifying constraints and criteria for desired qualities of the solution, developing a design plan, producing and testing models or prototypes, selecting among alternative design features to optimize the achievement of design criteria, and refining design ideas based on the performance of a prototype or simulation.
>
> (NRC Framework, 2012, p. 68–69)

Practice 7: Engaging in Argument from Evidence

The study of science and engineering should produce a sense of the process of argument necessary for advancing and defending a new idea or an explanation of a phenomenon and the norms for conducting such arguments. In that spirit, students should argue for the explanations they construct, defend their interpretations of the associated data, and advocate for the designs they propose.

(NRC Framework, 2012, p. 73)

Practice 8: Obtaining, Evaluating, and Communicating Information

Any education in science and engineering needs to develop students' ability to read and produce domain-specific text. As such, every science or engineering lesson is in part a language lesson, particularly reading and producing the genres of texts that are intrinsic to science and engineering.

(NRC Framework, 2012, p. 76)

Bibliography

Next Generation Science Standards: For States, By States. (2013). Appendix F—Science and Engineering Practices in the NGSS. Retrieved from www.nextgenscience.org/sites/ngss/files/Appendix%20F%20%20Science%20and%20Engineering%20Practices%20in%20the%20NGSS%20-%20FINAL%20060513.pdf

C3 Framework for Social Studies

Dimensions and Subsections

The C3 Framework is organized into the four dimensions, which support a robust social studies program rooted in inquiry.

Dimensions 2, 3, and 4 are further broken down into subsections. For example, Dimension 2, Applying Disciplinary Concepts and Tools, includes four subsections—civics, economics, geography, and history—which include descriptions of the structure and tools of the disciplines as well as the habits of mind common in those disciplines.

Dimension 1: Development of Questions and the Planning of Inquiries

With the entire scope of human experience as its backdrop, the content of social studies consists of a rich array of facts, concepts, and generalizations. The way to tie all of this content together is through the use of compelling and supporting questions.

Dimension 2: Applying Disciplinary Concepts and Tools

Working with a robust compelling question and a set of discrete supporting questions, teachers and students determine the kind of content they need in order to develop their inquiries. This process is an artful balancing act because the interplay between Dimensions 1 and 2 is dynamic: students access disciplinary knowledge both to develop questions and to pursue those questions using disciplinary concepts and tools.

Dimension 3: Evaluating Sources and Using Evidence

Having students gather, evaluate, and use a rich subset of those sources offers them opportunities to identify claims and counterclaims and to support those claims with evidence. Making and supporting evidence-based claims and counterclaims is key to student capacity to construct explanations and arguments.

Dimension 4: Communicating Conclusions and Taking Informed Action

These indicators demonstrate, those means include a range of venues and a variety of forms (e.g., discussions, debates, policy analyses, video productions, and portfolios). Moreover, the manner in which students work to create their solutions can differ. Students need opportunities to work individually, with partners, in small groups, and within whole class settings. Readiness for college, career, and civic life is as much about the experiences students have as it is about learning any particular set of concepts or tools. Thus, the learning environments that teachers create are critical to student success. Students will flourish to the extent that their independent and collaborative efforts are guided, supported, and honored.

Bibliography

National Council for the Social Studies (NCSS), *The College, Career, and Civic Life (C3) Framework for Social Studies State Standards: Guidance for Enhancing the Rigor of K–12 Civics, Economics, Geography, and History* (Silver Spring, MD: NCSS, 2013). Retrieved from www.socialstudies.org/system/files/c3/C3-Framework-for-Social-Studies.pdf